Tube Map Travels

Imitations, adaptations, and

explorations worldwide

Maxwell J. Roberts

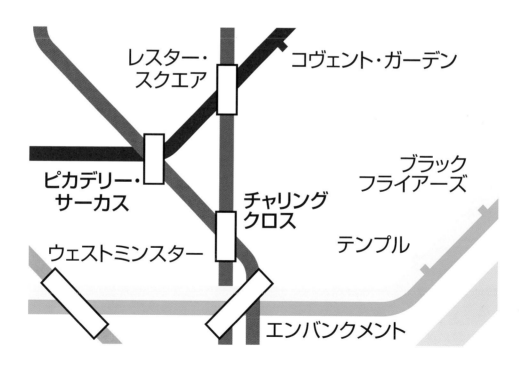

Capital Transport

First published 2019

ISBN 978-1-85414-444-7
Designed by the author
Typeset in ITC Johnston

Published by Capital Transport Publishing
www.capitaltransport.com

© Capital Transport Publishing, 2019

Author's website: www.tubemapcentral.com

About the Author

Maxwell Roberts received a bachelor's degree (1988) and a doctorate (1992) in psychology from the University of Nottingham. He taught at the Universities of Newcastle-upon-Tyne and St. Andrews, before accepting a lectureship at the University of Essex. He has researched extensively into intelligence, problem solving and reasoning, resulting in many scholarly publications. In 1999, with an evening to spare, he attempted to create a fantasy Underground map. Thus commenced an ongoing research programme to understand transport schematics, their effective design, and how to evaluate them using objective methodology. Along the way, numerous experimental, rule-breaking maps have charmed or infuriated the general public and his work has been exhibited internationally. He has designed and implemented usability studies on behalf of FWT Studios and Transport for London.

Image acknowledgements

All scanned maps are from the author's own collection with the following exceptions: p. 8/above left, The London Transport Museum; p. 8/above and top, Jim Whiting; p. 9/right, Jim Whiting; p. 14, Doug Rose; p. 28, Paul Mijksenaar. The designers/publishers/copyright holders of all unofficial original maps (and also designs with substantial, original design elements), that are still in copyright, were approached concerning inclusion of their work in this book. Thanks to those who replied in the affirmative: p. 4, © Michelin et Cie, 1996, authorisation No. GB121218; p. 18/above left, KLM Royal Dutch Airlines; p. 18/left, © Falk Verlag, D-73760 Ostfildern; p. 19, Underground Railways © Collins Bartholomew (1951), used with permission from HarperCollins Publishers Ltd; p. 20, Designed for Hachette Guides Bleus; p. 28, Paul Mijksenaar, www.mijksenaar.com; p. 39, Lets Go Inc; p. 55, Adrian Everett; p. 73, © Michelin et Cie, 2018, authorisation No. GB121218; p. 75, © Michelin et Cie, 2018, authorisation No. GB121218; p. 77, Martin Nöllenburg and Soeren Nickel; p. 80, Jug Cerovic, www.inat.fr; p. 81, Mike Hall, www.thisismikehall.com; p. 83, David Sherriff/Quickmap, www.quickmap.com; p. 85, Jug Cerovic, www.inat.fr; p. 86, Zero per Zero studios, www.zeroperzero.com; p. 89, Sameboat; p. 90, Andrew Smithers, www.projectmapping.co.uk; p. 93, Jonathan Fisher, www.massingbird.com; p. 94, Jonathan Farrow; back cover/third from top, © Michelin et Cie, 2018, authorisation No. GB121218. The maps on the following pages were designed and created by the author: pp. 78, 82, 84, 87, 88, 91, 92, 95 and back cover/fourth from top.

Special thanks to

Sietske de Groot, Chris Evans, John Ingham, Peter Lloyd, Mark Ovenden, Doug Rose and Jim Whiting.

Cover photograph by Ron Suffield

Contents

Preface

IN 2001, I COMMENCED WORK on my book: *Underground Maps After Beck* (2005), which gave the history of London designs from 1960 to the early 21st century. As part of my research, enthusiast Peter Lloyd generously allowed me access to his astonishing collection of historic urban rail maps. Amongst these, one item particularly caught my eye: an unofficial design of the London Underground, produced by an American cartographic company, intended to be added to a Filofax.

I was astonished. I had been so thoroughly conditioned into expecting Underground maps to be officially created, with a standardised look-and-feel that has been familiar to Londoners for decades, that it had not occurred to me that other versions might have been published. Different design rules and priorities might be adopted, transforming the appearance. The map that had surprised me so much was not well-executed, but that was not the point: I had seen something that was old and taken for granted – and perhaps a little bit stale – being reincarnated as something new. What else might be possible?

That map initiated a series of events which really did change my life, leading to my next book: *Underground Maps Unravelled* (2012), which explored the fundamentals of urban rail maps and the nature of effective information

design. However, the immediate consequence was that I started collecting unofficial London Underground maps, for example included in tourist guides and on folding street maps, as well as examples published on the Internet. The majority were acquired from specialist, secondhand and international bookshops. There must be at least 300 in my collection.

Why collect unofficial Underground maps? The official ones are well-documented, and acquiring these requires simply to locate and purchase them and then tick off each item on a list. Nobody knows how many unofficial designs have been created, and tourist publications are inherently disposable – who needs a 20-year-old guide to London? Hence older maps, which were comparatively rare to begin with, are difficult to track down, making the discovery of a hitherto unknown gem all the more delightful.

There is a more serious point to collecting these maps. Their existence raises awareness of the diverse solutions available for the problem of how to show information and sometimes highlights cultural differences between countries. Showing the same network in different ways offers a fairly controlled way of evaluating alternative approaches. For example, the official method of flagging interchanges (linked circles) is open to criticism: users may make unwarranted inferences from the configurations about ease-of-transfer between lines. Unofficial maps enable us to see alternative methods.

One organisation that might disagree with me about the benefits of unofficial London Underground maps is, of course, *Transport for London* (TfL). Many of the maps in my collection are thinly disguised copies of official versions, and although there are others that are more carefully camouflaged, their origins are still clear. As copyright violations, each of these represents the loss of licensing income to TfL. Furthermore, many of them have quite serious usability issues, or even mistakes, and one can only imagine the time and effort necessary for station staff to

Left: *The map that started it all. Streetwise Maps created various unofficial designs of the London Underground for many years, this is from 1996. Note the non-45° diagonals, rotated text and parks. © Michelin et Cie, 1996*

Above right: *Another inspiration; this German design from 2004 has barely a straight line in sight, but more radical alternatives are possible with a curvilinear design.*

Lower right: *The author's 2007* Curvy Tube Map *divided the public, with some liking its flowing organic feel, but with others objecting to its apparent lack of discipline and its perceived disorder.*

assist bemused passengers who have become thoroughly lost as a result. Publishers who sell such maps in the UK can expect to receive strongly worded cease-and-desist letters from TfL solicitors. Farther afield, international copyright violations are expensive and difficult to pursue.

From a design point of view, the world would definitely be a poorer place without these maps, and some of the more interesting ones point towards fruitful avenues of exploration. The author's own design; *Curvy Tube Map*, which achieved some notoriety, was inspired by a German creation. The original was let down by its execution, but the potential of using alternative design rules was clear. Overall, the maps in this book might be troublesome in certain quarters but nonetheless form a legitimate body of work for the design historian to research, understand, and document. For people who have purchased and attempted to use them, they are no less valid than the official designs: to them, they are 'the Underground map'.

With the rise of the Internet, a very different type of unofficial design has surfaced. Many people, including the author, have expressed dissatisfaction with recent versions of the official Underground map, or are simply bored with it and, equipped with computer power that would have been unheard of a few decades ago, try and do something about it. The result has been a minor industry of experimental DIY Underground maps. Some people seek improvement within the standard design rules – horizontal and vertical lines, and 45° diagonals. Others attempt more radical redesigns using unusual methodology, for example, different angles, concentric circles and spokes, or else no straight lines at all, while others deliberately create bizarre parodies in which usability is the least of their concerns.

For the first time, this book charts over one hundred years of unofficial Underground maps and explores the technological, political and commercial background that motivated their creation, and has resulted in their ever-increasing numbers in recent years. It also considers the wider issues of intellectual property, copyright and the nature of original design, along with showcasing some of the truly creative works that have been devised.

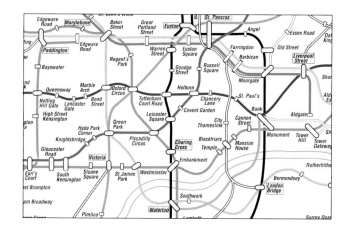

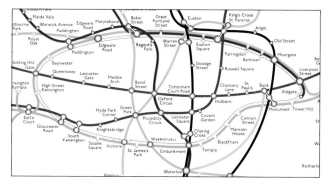

A note about terminology. Mathematical terms are used here to describe the basic design rules. The Underground standard – four angles of straight line (horizontal, vertical, and 45° diagonals) – is known as *octolinear*: at any given point a designer is permitted to move a pen in one of eight different directions. If there are unequal intervals between angles (e.g., horizontal, vertical, and 60° diagonals) then this is known as *irregular octolinear*. A design with just two angles is *tetralinear*, three angles is *hexalinear*, five angles is *decalinear*, and so on. If straight lines are permitted at any angle, the design is *multi-linear*, and if no straight lines are permitted, only curves, then it is *curvilinear*.

A note about sizes. The majority of third-party designs in this book were printed in standard-sized paperbacks and are reproduced as close as practical to their original sizes. Where the dimensions of the originals exceed the size of a printed page in this book, approximate measurements are given in brackets at the end of the caption.

Jostling for Position

TRAVEL BY TRAIN IN LONDON was not easy at the beginning of the 20th Century, with no fewer than sixteen different railway companies competing for business. Amongst the oldest of these were the main line operators. They generally focused on providing long-distance trains from London to the rest of the UK but, sometimes grudgingly, also offered local services. The first companies commenced operation in the 1830s and their networks were largely complete 50 years later. They conveyed passengers through London's growing suburbs in the open air, along viaducts and embankments, or through cuttings, with only the occasional tunnel. This led to their exclusion from the very centre of London, requiring large termini on its periphery, and resulting in inconvenience for passengers, most of them needing to make further arrangements to complete their journeys.

The second wave of railways were the first Underground lines. These were built in relatively shallow trenches along city streets, which were then covered and resurfaced. Even so, with construction being expensive and disruptive, these did not enter central London: they merely orbited it and linked the terminus stations of the main line railways. They were mainly built during the 1860s to 1880s and formed today's Circle, District, Hammersmith & City and Metropolitan Lines of the London Underground.

With technological developments, most notably the Greathead tunnelling shield, mechanical lifts and electric traction, it finally became financially viable for trains to enter central London – via deep tubes underground. The City & South London Railway (part of today's Northern Line) commenced operating in 1890. By 1907, five tube lines crossed central London, owned by three different companies. The largest of these, the *Underground Electric Railways of London Company* (UERL) owed its existence to American mass transit magnate, Charles Tyson Yerkes. He had taken control of the Metropolitan District Railway (today's District Line), and financed construction of the Charing Cross, Euston & Hampstead and also the Great Northern, Piccadilly & Brompton Railways (part of today's Northern Line and today's Piccadilly Line respectively) as well as the completion of the Baker Street & Waterloo Railway (part of today's Bakerloo Line).

The early tube lines, all created via private investment, generally performed poorly financially. Some effectively were bankrupt the moment they turned their wheels. Their appeal to surface-travelling passengers had been over-estimated, and the emergence of competition, such as petrol buses and electric trams, underestimated. Unlike the main line railways, they did not have profitable long distance traffic to subsidise the shortfall. Their original business models conceptualised them as self-contained, independent railways, with other modes of travel either irrelevant or else dangerous competition to be shunned. Through tickets between them were certainly not on offer, and the still-standing (now disused) adjacent pair of ticket offices at Oxford Circus for the Baker Street & Waterloo and the Central London Railways reminds us of the waste that can result from company rivalry.

From the point of view of railway cartography, the early situation was absurd, with competing independent companies emphasising their own services at the expense of rivals, sometimes excluding them altogether. Colour-coding, where used, was there to emphasise the 'correct' choice of railway company, rather than assist passengers in planning long and complex journeys. Furthermore, because most operators were highly localised, their maps reflected this, with the extent of London, apparently, being defined strictly by the end of the line.

There was nothing special about human beings one hundred years ago that meant that they were better-equipped than ourselves to cope with confusion and poor information design: witness Jerome K. Jerome's hilarious accounts of attempting to travel by train. There was clearly a perceived demand for improvements and, with railway

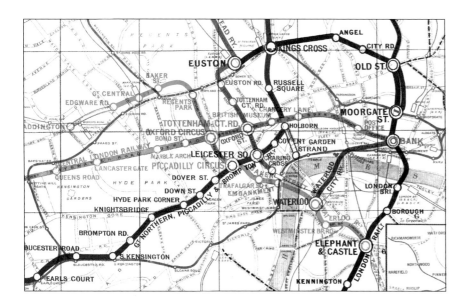

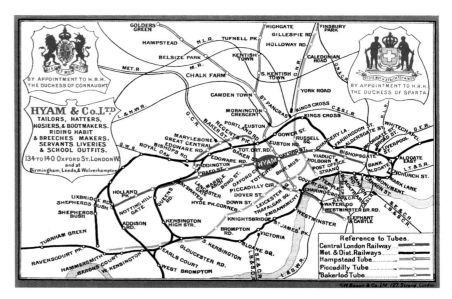

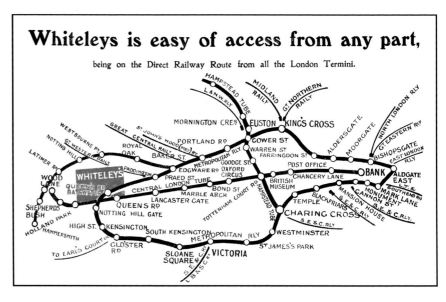

companies reluctant to promote rivals on their maps, it was inevitable that outsiders would create alternatives. These were aimed not only at residents but also visitors to London: with the rise of tourism, the ever increasing numbers of travellers were being offered books about popular destinations – *Baedeker* published its first comprehensive guide to London (in German) in 1862 – and the futility of binding sixteen official railway maps into these, all different shapes and sizes, would have been obvious. Thus, the railway companies themselves created an environment in which independent cartographers could flourish, some aiming for greater network coverage or else attempting to improve clarity, while others, focusing on a specific destination, assembled a subset of railways that best served it. One of the key elements of modern urban rail map design – the colour-coding of lines – was independently pioneered on a 1907 map published by the *Evening News* and drawn by George Philip and Son.

The *Evening News* map highlighted a certain type of railway: the deep-level tube lines of inner London, irrespective of ownership and rivalry. The UERL would undoubtedly have been unhappy that its District Railway did not receive equal promotion alongside its tube lines. Irrespective of this, independently-produced maps put the railway companies at risk of losing control of their maps – a key element of their marketing and publicity. The worsening financial position of the tube lines created the solution to this and, in 1908, certain operators reached agreement on joint ticketing and marketing. Henceforth, the UERL lines, alongside the Central London, City & South London, Great Northern & City, and Metropolitan Railways would pool resources and collectively be known as the UNDERGROUND, and be shown on one single official map.

Above left: *The 1907 Evening News London Tube Map introduced unique colours for each tube line, improving clarity compared with p. 6. However, the other electric railways in London were neglected. Subsequent Evening News maps used the official colours introduced in 1908. [64 by 50 cm]*

Above and top: *In the early days of Underground lines many advertisers created their own maps that showed only those railways useful for visiting their premises, hence networks often differed from official ones. The Hyam map is from 1907 and the Whiteleys one from between 1908 and 1912.*

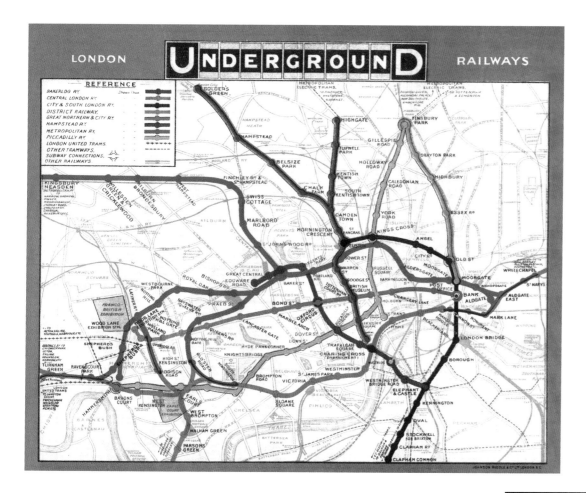

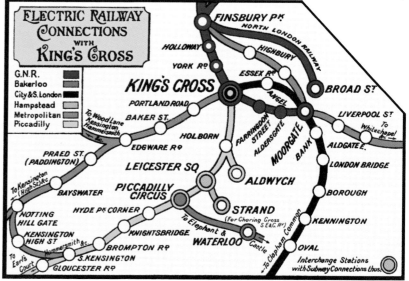

The *unification map* was significant for many reasons. By combining forces, the companies behind it had executed a very successful land-grab in terms of mapping London. Although there was still a multitude of railway maps by other companies focusing on the areas that they served (many of these having little or no Underground presence) only the unification map showed comprehensive coverage of central London. It highlighted direct services to and from tourist attractions, theatres, shops, offices and other important destinations, and all could be reached with just one ticket. If the publisher of a tourist guide or street map of London had to choose just one official railway map, the Underground design would be the one most likely to be of use to most readers. Simultaneously, the unification map defined the core set of key lines that served this area. For example, the Waterloo & City Railway declined to be unified, despite being a tube railway, and it was destined (like all the other railways of London) to be pushed into the background. Furthermore, this widely-publicised map would generate an expectation amongst the general public that the components of the Underground network should be shown together as one single functioning unit, depicted in officially sanctioned colours, putting an end to some of the less coherent assemblages of lines by third parties.

Above: *The first officially branded map that marked the unification of the various Underground railways (1908). It included important streets, parks, landmarks, and also water. The colour-coding still partly reflected company ownership rather than the routes taken by the trains, hence the awkward transitions where Metropolitan and District railways met. Other railways were shown in the background. The line colour scheme lasted until the First World War, but colour was not used on Underground signage at the time and so changes would not have caused too much confusion. [27 by 22 cm]*

Right: *Main line railways were barely shown on official Underground maps, if at all, but many of these depended on the Underground for distributing their passengers and this led to the creation of their own maps to show connections. The 1916 Great Northern Railway map included this inset for their arrivals transferring at Finsbury Park, King's Cross and Broad Street, assisting people who wished to travel to west and south London. However, the Underground in north London competed with Great Northern suburban services and many lines are conspicuous by their absence.*

The unification map was not particularly innovative from a usability or aesthetic perspective: it was topographically accurate and showed major surface features. Nonetheless, the publicity value for its railways was immense. However, despite its utility for third-party publishers, the market for independent maps was not quite extinguished. With the Underground comprising much less than half the total railway mileage in London, there would still be demand from people who wished to see the network in the context of the full extent of London's railways, and such maps continued to be sold as unofficial, standalone publications. Furthermore, as the Underground continued to expand,

the priority to show the entire network, all the way from Watford in the north (reached in 1917) to Morden in the south (reached in 1926) inevitably required simplification in the form of omitted surface details, as well as some topographical distortion. In theory, this should not affect journey planning (i.e., identifying the best route from Station A to Station B) but for people unfamiliar with London surface information can serve a useful orienting purpose, setting the railways in context, showing their coverage, and enabling the most appropriate stations to be identified. Hence, some tourist guides included unofficial Underground maps which had a more detailed overview

Right: *The Daily Telegraph Map of London's Railways dates between 1915 and 1920 and was designed by Geographia. The only surface details shown are the River Thames and other major water features, parks, and tram routes. Official Underground maps squeezed out many independent ventures but there was still a niche for maps that showed all of London's railways. Unfortunately, use of two colours, presumably owing to the need for wartime economies, inhibits clarity. The inclusion of additional surface features would have exacerbated this problem. [100 by 76 cm]*

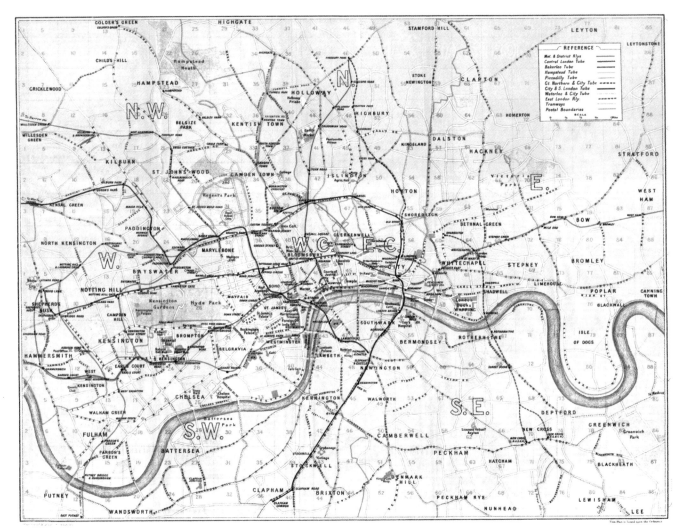

Left: *From the English Blue Guide for London of 1918 (still titled Muirhead's London and Its Environs), an intricately drawn street map with Underground lines printed in colour, alongside main line railways and tram lines. It was included as a supplementary package of maps in a slip at the back of the book. Only central and inner London are shown, as expected for a tourist guide, but many streets have been omitted. Even so, the clear parks and river emphasise the context of the railway lines, hence assisting a tourist in making sense of an unfamiliar city. [41 by 31 cm]*

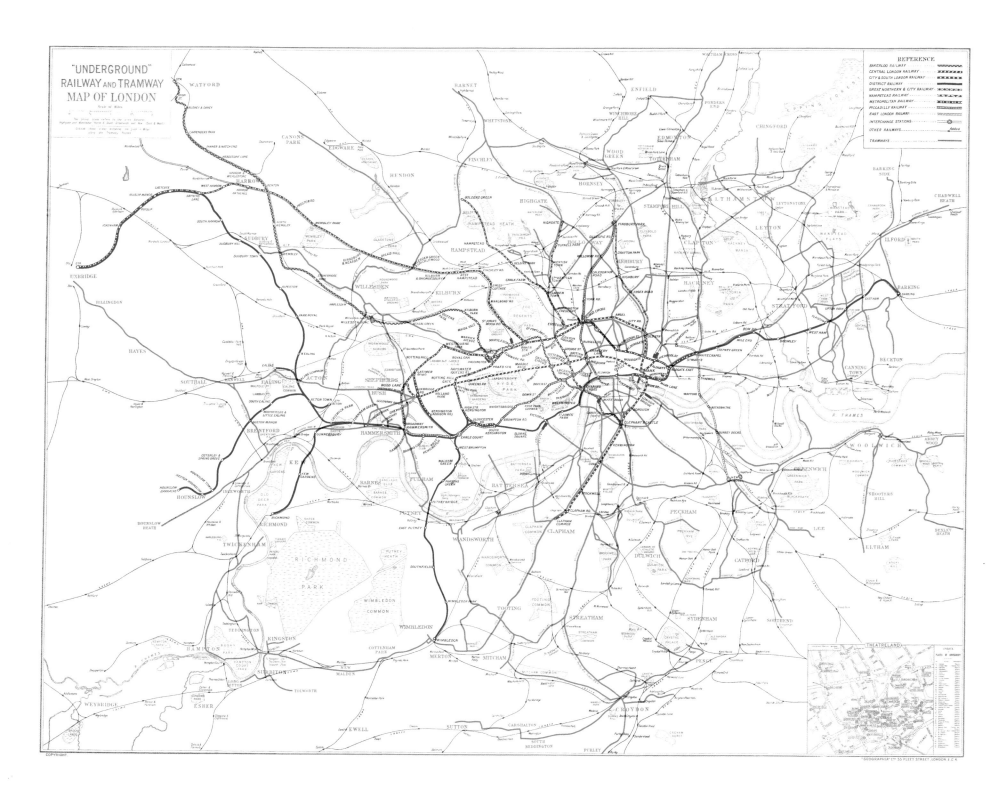

"UNDERGROUND"
RAILWAY AND TRAMWAY
MAP OF LONDON

REFERENCE

BAKERLOO RAILWAY
CENTRAL LONDON RAILWAY
CITY & SOUTH LONDON RAILWAY
DISTRICT RAILWAY
GREAT NORTHERN & CITY RAILWAY
HAMPSTEAD RAILWAY
METROPOLITAN RAILWAY
PICCADILLY RAILWAY
EAST LONDON RAILWAY
INTERCHANGE STATIONS
OTHER RAILWAYS
TRAMWAYS

11

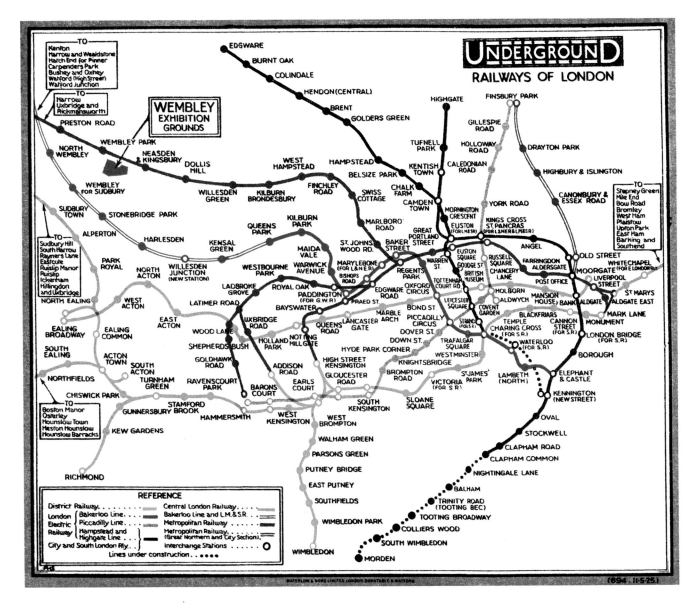

Left: 1925 Underground pocket map by Frederick Stingemore, in which the scale was compressed in the suburbs in order to show a reasonable proportion of the network legibly. For example, the Morden extension to the Northern Line has been noticeably squeezed upwards. Hence, these maps communicated topographical impressions rather than absolute accuracy; useful enough to show the best stations for the Wembley Exhibition Grounds.

Right: Kennedy North's remarkable 1923 creation is an early example of a journey planner: a map intended for identifying a journey from A to B but not for geographical assistance in choosing these stations. In this case, A was the home station – already known to the user – and B was a station for the British Empire Exhibition. North surmised that topographical accuracy would be irrelevant for this purpose, and in the process drafted a perfectly circular Inner Circle (today's Circle Line). He included all railways useful for travelling to Wembley, irrespective of company rivalry. [75 by 50 cm]

of the network's relationship with geography than could be obtained from the compact official maps that were distributed to the general public.

By the mid 1920s, official maps had reduced scale and few surface details so that the expanding network could be shown. From 1925 to 1932, pocket maps were drawn by Frederick Stingemore and, for the first two years, even the River Thames was absent. Even so, many Underground extremities could not be included and had to be boxed out. Main line railways were expunged but even tramways operated by the UERL were excluded. Hence the maps gave a very selective view of travel in London, with limited utility in the east and south – where the Underground only had a token presence. For tourist guides, whose users would not be expected to venture far from the centre, such an approach might still be adequate so that official maps were used in many of these, either in monochrome or as a separate colour sheet bound into the book.

Up until the 1930s, Underground cartography was only sporadically innovative and designers seemed to pay little attention to work that preceded them. The lack of progress was highlighted in 1923 by a remarkable creation by Kennedy North. Here, a special event provided the impetus and the designer invented a *journey planner*. With this, topographical fidelity was unnecessary, permitting simplified line trajectories and topographical distortion, concepts that would become of key importance for urban rail map creation in the future. Before 1933, limitations in official Underground cartography inspired many creative alternatives by independent designers. However, this situation was soon to reverse and the UERL would spawn imitation rather than innovation.

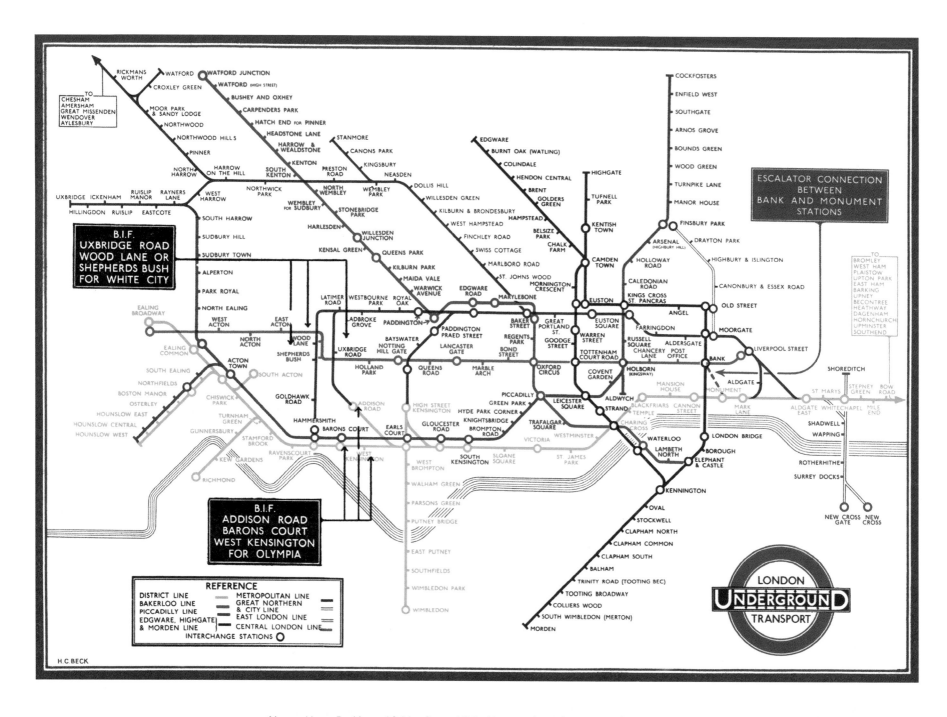

Above: *Henry Beck's card folder, first published in 1933, showed the Underground network in its entirety, for the first time, as a compact diagram with simple straight lines. This provided a perfect eye-catching visual for guide books seeking to provide information on London's railways, even though its coverage was incomplete. This is a second edition version, also published in 1933. Many maps were overprinted, often unofficially, to advertise special events. This one is for the British Industries Fair.*

Chapter Two

Swimming Against the Tide

Below: *To the author's knowledge, this is the first overseas excursion for Beck's diagrammatic map, appearing as a separate page glued into the German Grieben Reiseführer guide of 1934. Other than some useful translations, the design appears to be unaltered. Showing the network in monochrome without any reference to, or differentiation of, individual Underground lines would have made using this map a challenge for planning journeys, especially for people who might have been unfamiliar with the network.*

THE NETWORK OF UNDERGROUND LINES in London was finally tamed by Henry Beck, whose diagrammatic map was published in 1933. This combined a number of schematisation methods that had already been used extensively both on London Underground signage *and* publicity, including omitted surface features, distorted scale, use of straight lines at limited angles and simplified line trajectories. His inventiveness is often overstated at the expense of his design skills. He did not create any new mapping techniques. Instead, his great achievement was a balanced, coherent, simplified depiction of the *entire* network, without any previous attempts by others to guide him. This was all achieved without excessive topographical distortion, cushioning users from the surprise of seeing the whole Underground as a diagram for the first time.

Beck's map seems to have been well-received right from the start, although contemporary critiques of his work have not been unearthed. From the point of view of mapping London, this modern, elegant image was, indeed, a game-changer and many guidebooks quickly adopted it. The very first edition of the diagram was bound into copies of the 1933 London *Blue Guide* (English edition, the sister French publication continued to use its own monochrome topographical map). The first overseas outing seems to have been in 1934, with a monochrome version glued into the German *Grieben Reiseführer*. With a powerful image of the railways of central London, available in colour or monochrome gratis to publishers (who would have only needed to pay for reproduction costs), the stage was set for world conquest. However, the process was not entirely smooth and there were a number of hiccups along the way; adaptations of the Beck design began to appear – the earliest known example in 1937 – and at least some of these caused distress to officials at London Transport (UERL had become state-owned and was simultaneously renamed in 1933).

Why go to the trouble of including an adaptation of the official Underground map in a brochure or a tourist guide? This would have required the time and effort of creating (by hand) and photographing a new drawing and preparing the necessary colour separations, so that a printing plate could be prepared for each colour. Judging by the designs discovered, the problem seems to be that although the necessary artwork was available from the organisation behind the official map, the six colours used (down to five in 1937, then up to seven in 1949) were not necessarily the ones that the publisher of the tourist guide was able or willing to use. Hence, many unofficial maps exist with unusual colour-coding which would not have been a source of significant confusion for tourists until the late 1930s, when signage on the Underground commenced using line colours for navigation.

Grieben Verlag, Berlin

Leop. Kraatz, Berlin.

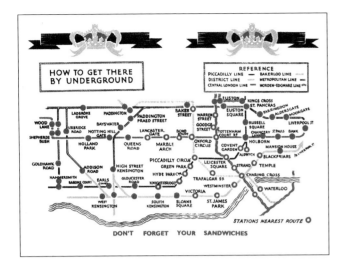

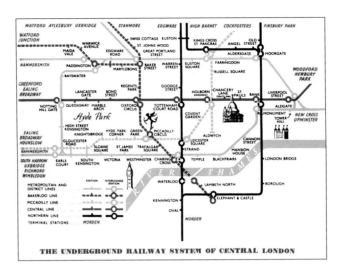

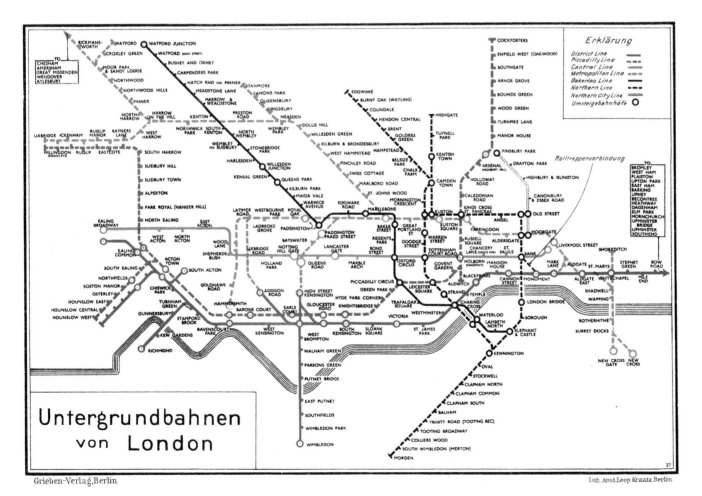

Far left: *The first home-grown adaptation of the Underground map seems to have been included as part of a tiny Millers' Mutual Association brochure for the 1937 coronation celebrations. Printed in three colours, the booklet befittingly extols the virtue of bread products throughout.*

Lower left: *The first international adaptation followed soon after. The 1938 Grieben Reiseführer now included a redrawn version, also in three colours. Even if this had been authorised, London Transport would have been unlikely to be happy with a strangely crooked branch down to Hammersmith.*

Above near left: *An adaptation that was published after the Second World War, in 1947, as part of the London Past and Present brochure produced for the Travel Association of the U.K. of Great Britain and N. Ireland. Beck's third version of the diagram (p. 21) has been modified, reproduced in four colours and a few landmarks added. The italic lettering denoting line termini contrasts with the more sober official Johnston lettering for the station names.*

Below: *The 1951 Festival of Britain attracted visitors to its different venues from all over the UK but this map is particularly bemusing. The circular Circle Line has been used before (p. 13) but not as an inverted mirror image, sending people walking between the South Bank and the Pleasure Gardens in entirely the wrong directions.*

Right: *Wembley is several miles from central London so major events led to numerous how-to-get-there guides. The Jehovah's Witnesses Clean Worship Assembly, running August 1–5, 1951, warranted booking the stadium. Hence, even religious organisations needed their own Underground maps, as shown by this more-conventional three-colour diagram. [24 by 24 cm]*

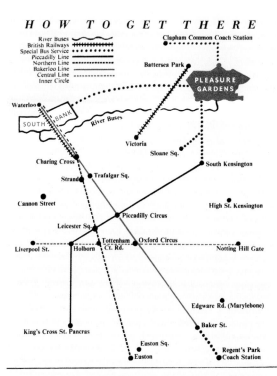

FESTIVAL OF BRITAIN INFORMATION CENTRE
SWAN & EDGAR BUILDING · PICCADILLY CIRCUS · LONDON · W.1
Telephone: REGent 0531/6

FESTIVAL GARDENS LIMITED
INFORMATION OFFICE · BATTERSEA PARK
Telephone: BATtersea 6444

Publicity Arts Ltd, London, WC2

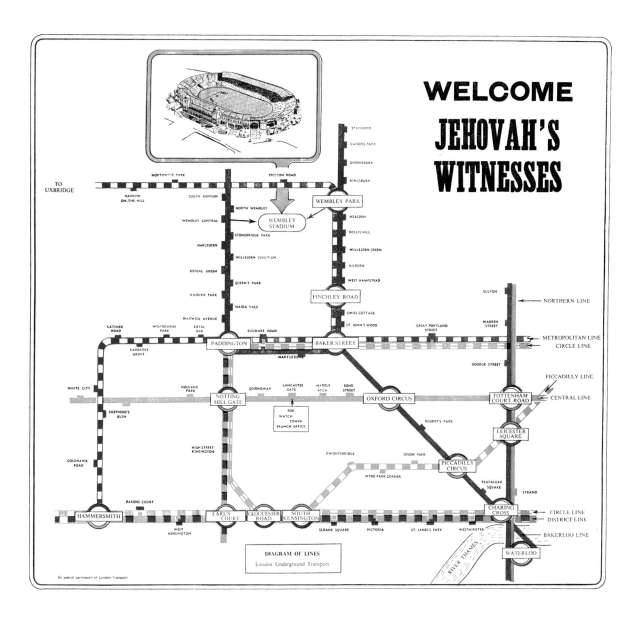

Another reason for dissatisfaction with the official diagram might have been its sparseness, showing none of the landmarks that might be sought by tourists. For a compact design, festooning it with places of interest would destroy the essence of its usability. Its prime purpose has always been as a tool for planning journeys between stations that have already been chosen, not as a means for selecting these: users were expected to consult other maps for this. However, this did not prevent some unofficial derivations from being embellished.

For special events at particular venues, official maps were sometimes overprinted to show how to get to these. Alternatively, a specific map might be created showing just the key routes, occasionally appearing so dramatically different from official versions that even London residents might have trouble relating the two together.

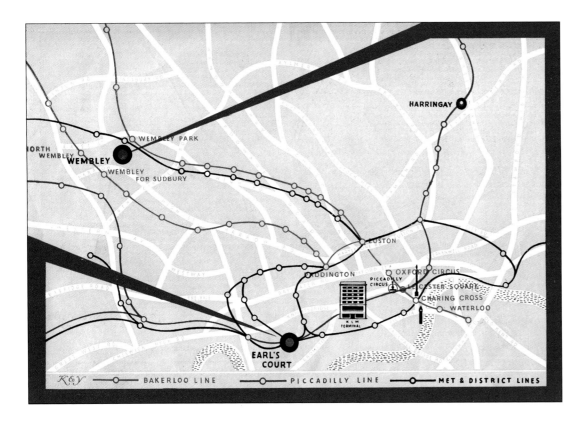

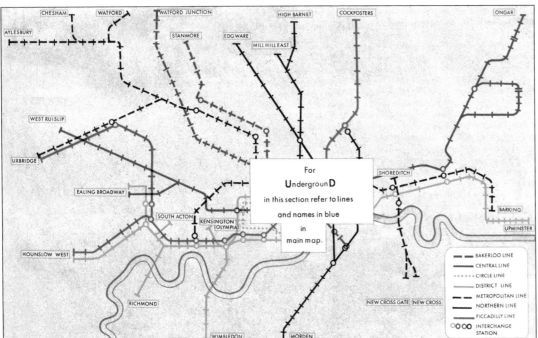

The diagrammatic concept itself does not have universal appeal, precisely because of the possibility of inaccurate topography. Many users complain about its potential to cause the selection of inappropriate stations, or even the planning of inefficient journeys. The argument, that they should carry two maps – a diagrammatic rail map and a topographical street map – using each according to is strengths, cuts little ice: the preference is for no distortion at all. Beck's original work would have caused little upset, but his later designs became more and more abstract, moving far away from reality (e.g., p. 21).

The preference for topographical accuracy led many publishers to create their own Underground maps, also sometimes including major streets along with landmarks. For visitors to London, unfamiliar with its disorganised

Above left: *Wembley again features as a tourist destination, this time on a geographical map as part of a KLM Airlines brochure produced for the 1948 Olympic games. Its sober post-war colours are an intriguing contrast compared with the more exuberant design on p. 13. Three routes are shown from Paddington to Earl's Court but one of these had been abandoned during the Second World War, and another required a change of stations at Hammersmith.*

Right: *The 1951 map from the Bartholomew Pocket Atlas Guide to London appears to be topographical but in fact uses the same compression techniques as the map on p. 12; a true successor to Frederick Stingemore's work. Hence the centre is large enough to be legible and the outer suburbs are pulled inwards to fit. The variable scale causes a lot of compression in northwest and northeast London. In reality the Hainault loop of the Central Line covers a greater area than the Circle Line.*

Left: *An uncomfortable creation, by German cartographer Falk, was included on their 1966 street map of London. It cannot decide whether it is a topographical map or a diagram. Without station names its use was limited but showing line destinations might help passengers choose the correct direction of travel.*

UNDERGROUND RAILWAYS

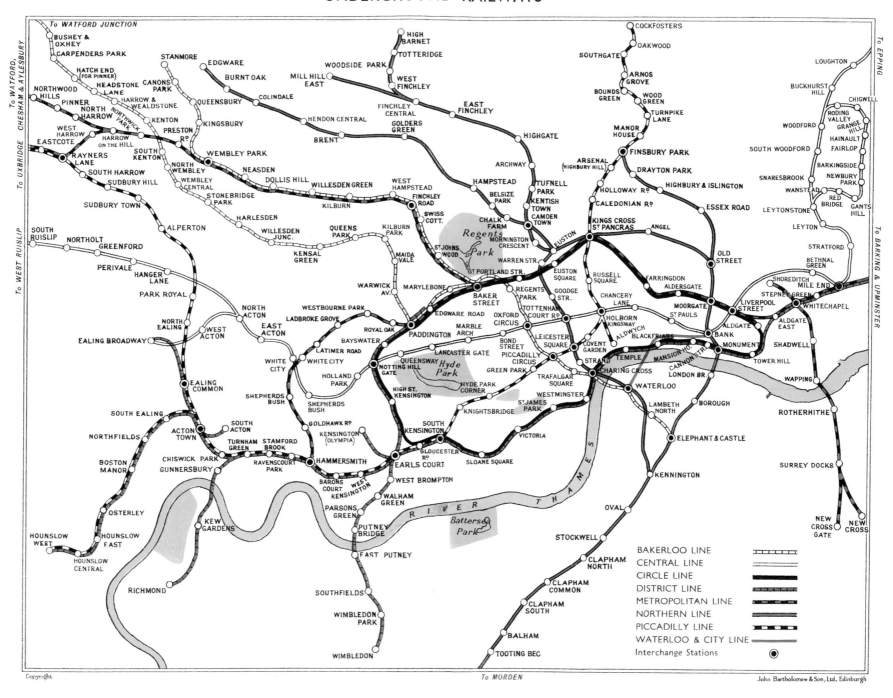

layout, it is likely they would benefit from topographical assistance to help orient themselves to the relationships between city streets, landmarks and the deeply hidden Underground railways linking them. However, to create such maps required trade-offs that limited their utility. Beck created his diagram precisely because he perceived clarity issues with topographical maps, and the only ways in which a compact version for London can be salvaged is either by restricting its coverage to the centre of the city (from which few tourists would be expected to stray) or else by removing so many surface details that those very features that are supposed to be useful to London visitors, to help them orientate or select the appropriate stations, are nowhere to be seen. Hence, the clarity of a diagram outweighs the perceived costs, provided that it does not compromise journey planning.

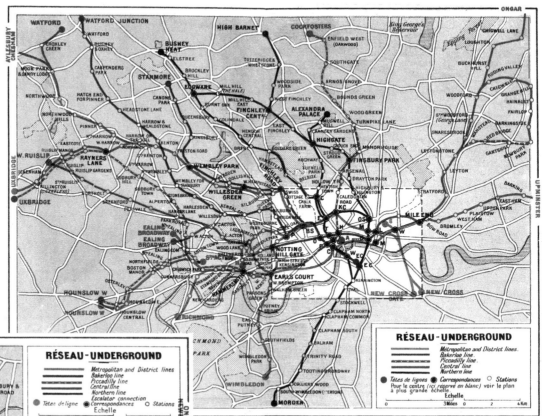

Above and left: *The problem of showing an extensive network can be solved by using an inset and two maps at different scale. The French Blue Guide of 1952 attempted this, with these two designs at opposite ends of the book. The selected major roads are not named and there are few landmarks. Some Northern Line extensions, shown as operational, were never completed.*

Above right: *Beck's third style of map considerably reduced the use of diagonals, increasing topographical distortion. The Inner Circle was coloured yellow and named the Circle Line in 1949.*

Near and far right: *In the 1950s, use of Underground maps by Foldex street maps began with the inclusion of official monochrome versions. These were subsequently redrawn by Foldex for colour printing; the 1957 version resembles official maps but the Northern and Piccadilly Lines are both dark blue.*

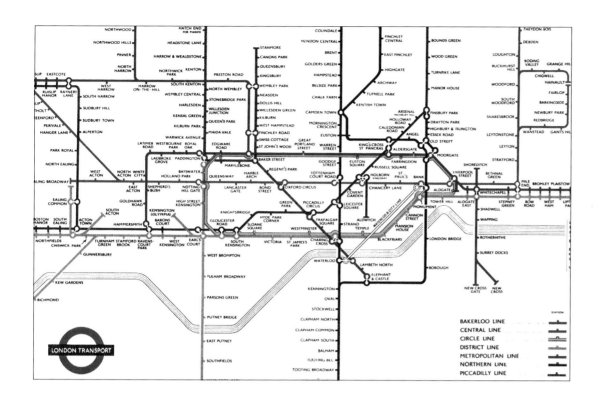

How did London Transport officials respond when they discovered unauthorised modifications to their diagram? One exchange of archived memos and letters suggests that prime concerns included the accuracy of information, and the incorrect depiction of line colours. The sequence of designs by *Foldex* started innocently enough with an official monochrome version included on their 1950s maps of London. However, this soon took on a life of its own, gradually mutating for almost two decades. By the time it came to the notice of London Transport, in the form of a map created for the British Overseas Aircraft Corporation, it must have come as a shock. A.B. Beaumont, Publicity Officer for London Transport, fired off a rather pointed complaint to BOAC on the 26th February 1973:

'I am very disturbed by a small map of London of yours that has just come to hand.
In it is an Underground map that is 20 years old and as you can guess well out of date. Your publishers have also had

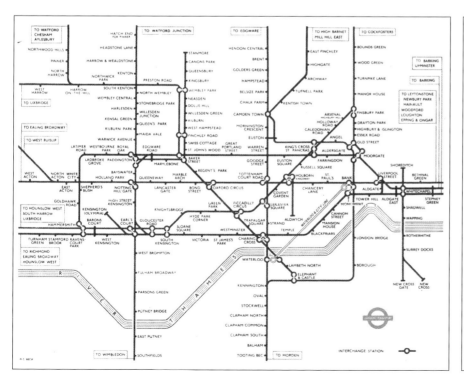

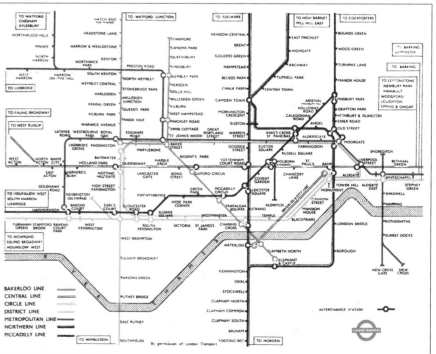

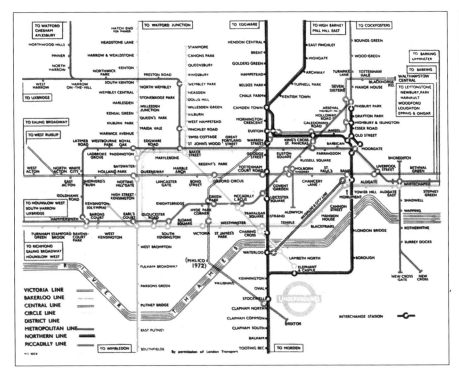

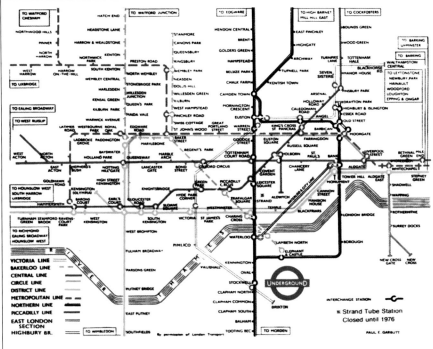

the impudence to draw in the New Victoria Line right across the map. Their choice of colours are most peculiar, blue for the Central Line and red for the Victoria Line.
Please draw this to their attention and tell them that they can have up to date artwork from us just for the asking.'

He was probably taken aback by the robustness of the response from Foldex:

'(...) There is nothing peculiar about the colouring for any one experienced in printing and publishing.
(...) No customer we know would agree to heavy extra charges to print one or two extra colours on a long run, just to change a small thin line or two – which the reader probably would not care less about anyway. (...)
We would welcome art work which would take our colour needs into account but we received diagrams some time back from this department (...) so imperfect in design that it was put away and we have never cared to ask for art work since (...).'

There might well be an element of protesting too much by the Foldex representative. Official Underground maps had been reproduced by many other publishers, apparently without difficulty, for decades. There was no intrinsic reason for a colour scheme that was quite so unhelpful. For example, red was available but the Central Line was shown in blue. The list of mistakes that London Transport identified on the 1973 map was impressive:

Underground serving Aylesbury (ceased 1962);
Northern City Line serving Finsbury Park (ceased 1964);
Metropolitan Line serving White City (closed 1959);
Many interchange stations omitted by the Circle Line.

Despite the initial angry exchange, the correspondence soon calmed down but it is interesting that there was never any mention of legal action. London Transport seemed anxious to go out of its way to rectify the situation, with offers of artwork to suit the needs of the publisher. The problems of printing in limited colours were not fully

Above left: *The* Foldex *map had acquired the Victoria Line by the 1970s, with an ungainly diagonal towards Brixton. The colour scheme is, at best, unhelpful. For example, three different blue lines meet at Holborn. The map is undated, but is almost certainly the version referred to in the text.*

Above: *The exchange of letters seems to have had some effect, with colours closer to official ones on this 1973* Foldex *redesign. However, new errors have crept in. Bizarrely, Paul Garbutt is credited. His first Underground map was issued in 1964, and he was not responsible for the 1940s base version of the* Foldex *designs in any way.*

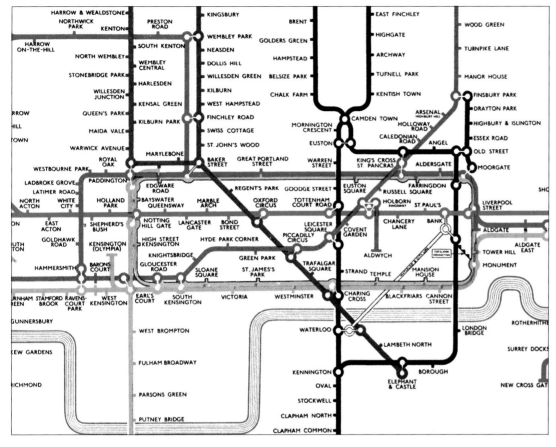

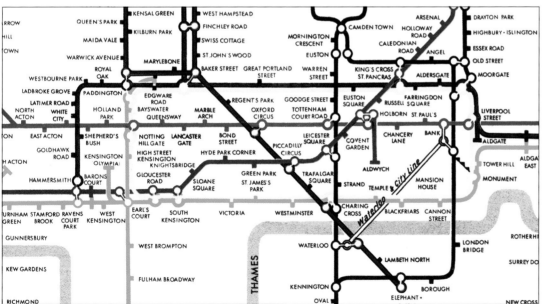

resolved and the final outcome (by now issued on behalf of British Airways) would not have been deemed a success. Although the colours had changed better to match official ones, correcting some of the errors resulted in others, such as White City Central Line station vanishing (this was separate from the Metropolitan Line station of the same name) and no indication that the Metropolitan Line still served Amersham.

Sterner words seem to have been reserved for German cartographer, Falk. Their 1950s folding maps of London included an Underground diagram which was based on Beck's fourth and final design (officially issued from 1954 to 1960) but redrawn for printing in five colours. By the time that it came to the attention of London Transport in 1971 it had been re-redrawn for four-colour printing and become yet another Victoria Line casualty. Unfortunately, only one letter survives but it contains enough details for the gaps to be filled in. This was from A.B. Beaumont to London Transport's solicitors, dated 9th August:

'(...) You will see they have offered to pay us £100 but, not unnaturally, want to continue with the maps they have produced. In my view this is totally unacceptable. Quite apart from the fact they have reproduced maps without our authority, these maps are, in fact, quite inaccurate and a travesty of our system.

Above left: *Henry Beck's fourth official design continued his quest to eradicate diagonals. First issued in 1954, the grid-like layout, complete with rectangular Circle Line, polarises commentators. Some praise its abstract minimalism, others complain about the most topographically distorting map ever issued by London Transport.*

Left: *The redrawing of the design by Falk, possibly in the 1950s, and presumably because it was desired to print in five colours rather than seven, is reasonably well-executed. It is set in Futura rather than the official Johnston lettering, but it is unlikely that a casual user would have noticed anything amiss.*

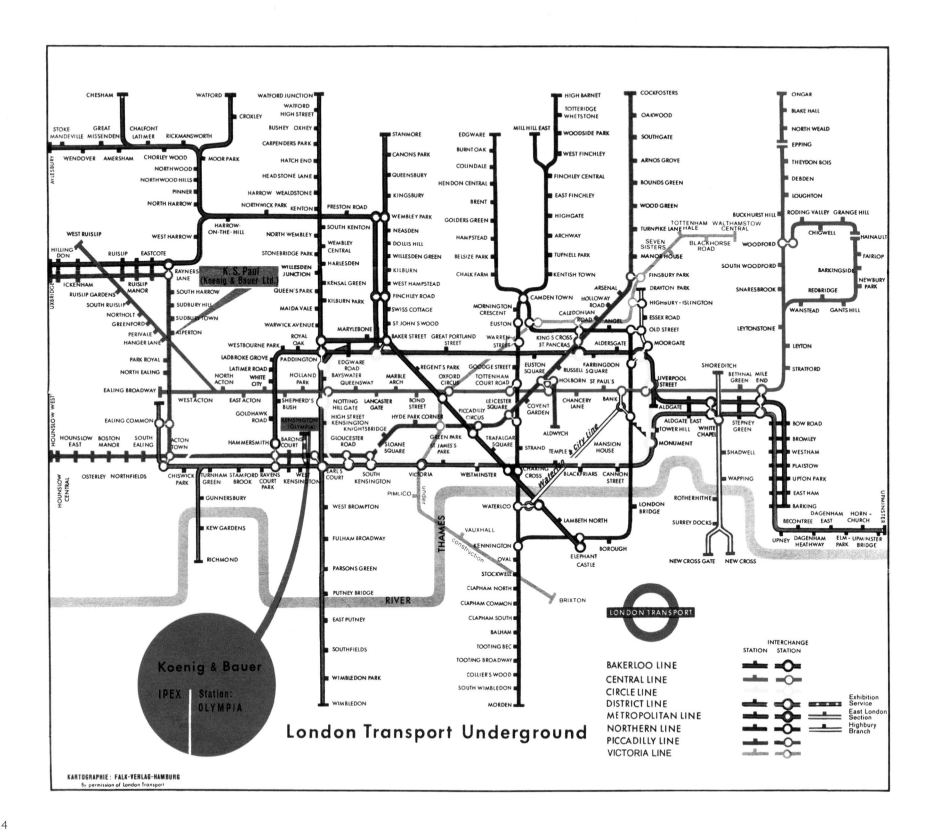

London Transport Underground

KARTOGRAPHIE: FALK-VERLAG-HAMBURG
By permission of London Transport

24

Left: *The Falk version of the map lasted for at least a decade. This version was produced for an exhibitor at the IPEX printing trade show, Olympia, 1971. Despite modifying their own drawings for four-colour printing, Falk made no attempt to accommodate the Victoria Line neatly, which ruins the overall appearance of the map.*

Above right: *While some publishers revamped obsolete designs to their detriment, in 1964 London Transport had commenced issuing elegant maps with improved topographical accuracy devised by Paul Garbutt. The version shown here was bound into the 1967 Ward Lock London Red Guide. By this time, official pocket maps had a grid added but versions printed for use by third parties were not cluttered in this way, giving them a cleaner appearance overall.*

Right: *The 1969 Stern Reiseführer, published by Axel Juncker, included a redrawing of the official 1960s map, presumably again because of colour – it is printed in five of these. Notably, the appearance of the design is subtly altered by changing the station markers from ticks to dots, anticipating the style of Massimo Vignelli's famous New York City Subway map by three years. The station names are set in Univers, a combination that gives the map a subtle international style.*

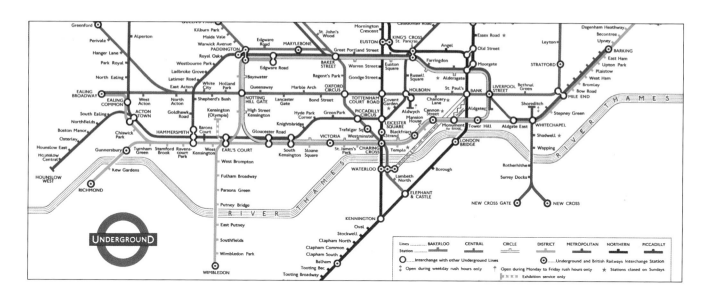

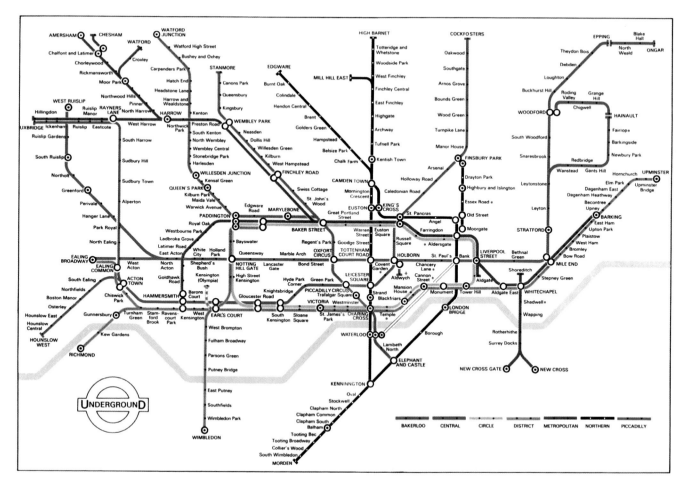

'(...) There should, of course, be no question of a royalty at all and I believe we only extracted a royalty from them on the last occasion as some sort of tangible admission of their guilt. In the normal way people wishing to reproduce our maps ask us for the artwork, quoting the dimensions, and we provide these entirely free of charge. (...) I would like to write to them again insisting that these rogue maps be withdrawn. I should be grateful for your help.'

Irrespective of the contents of the letter that was sent to Falk, it seems to have had the desired effect, because no subsequent outings for this design are known.

Perhaps the most galling aspect of the various unofficial redesigns of this era is the frequent proclamation that they were sanctioned "By permission of London Transport" implying an awareness of, and a condoning of, these works. Certainly, this would have given a bad impression of London Transport, but the generosity of the organisation was possibly partly to blame. Giving away artwork for free

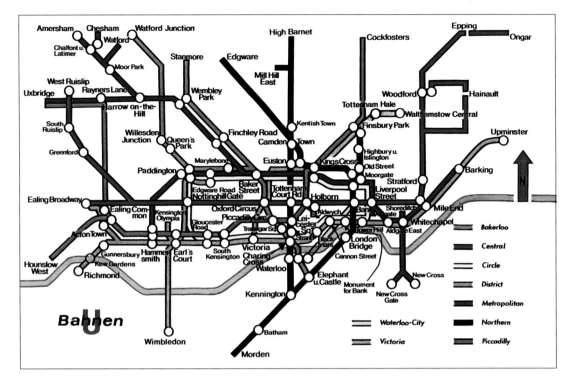

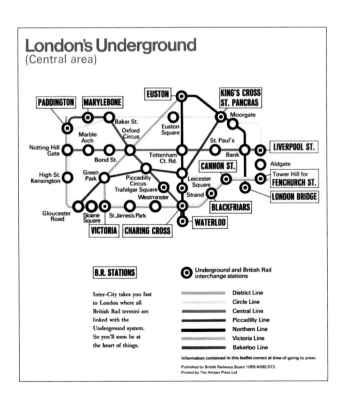

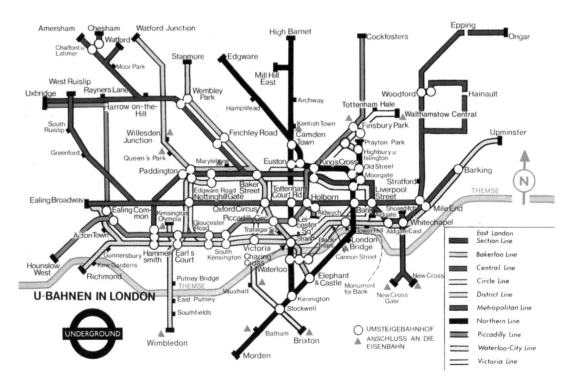

Left and below left: *A bizarre creation from the 1972 German Polyglott Große Reiseführer, which shows only major central stations, interchanges and destinations. Despite the whimsical appearance, it is clear that the base map is the official one on p. 25. The 1974 version was more anglicised, and the Victoria Line Brixton extension was added. The blue triangles, denoting British Rail interchanges, have been omitted from several stations.*

Far left: *Even British Rail was using its own version of the Underground map, rather than an official one, on this 1973 pamphlet encouraging people to visit London.*

Above right: *Another German derivation, this time from the 1977 Goldstadt-Reiseführer and printed in three colours. London was an early pioneer of consistently colour-coded lines: other networks were far slower to adopt this. Hence, non-UK publishers might appreciate less the need for constancy. Fortunately for tourists, cheaper colour printing would soon reduce the prevalence of such confusion.*

Right: *A cheaply produced postcard, with blurry photographs on a poorly drawn Underground map. As well as giving a bad impression of the Underground, unlicensed items were potentially depriving London Transport of income.*

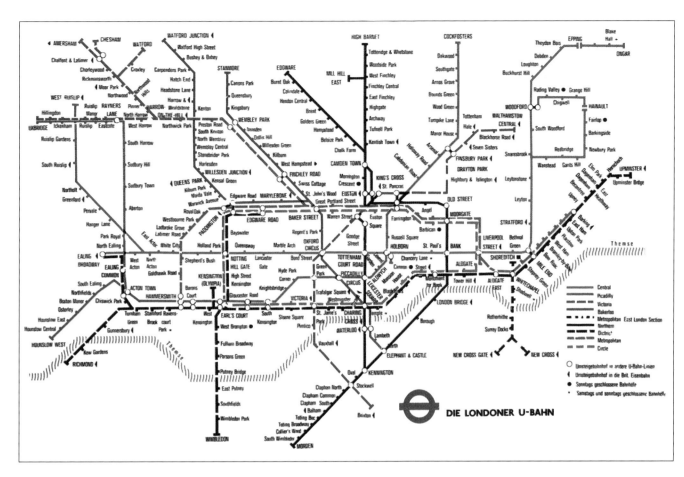

DIE LONDONER U-BAHN

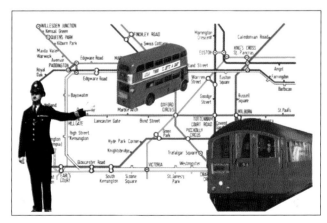

could be taken to imply a relaxed attitude to how it could be used and implicit permission to adapt it as necessary. Had payment been required, it might have been treated with more respect and perhaps publishers would have been more motivated to insist on the latest versions.

The 1970s drew to a close with officials at London Transport realising that they needed to take firmer steps to prevent continual abuses of their intellectual property. Publishers were corrupting designs and the supply of appropriately sized and coloured artwork to them, free of charge, was giving away prestige and credibility without necessarily accruing reciprocal benefits. There was also growing sales of counterfeit goods, with souvenir manufacturers benefitting from the map without London Transport receiving a share. There seemed to be a market for map-printed goods, implying potential to develop sources of income. Hence, the next decade was marked by a more commercial attitude to the Underground map but not yet with the backing of an effective policing machine.

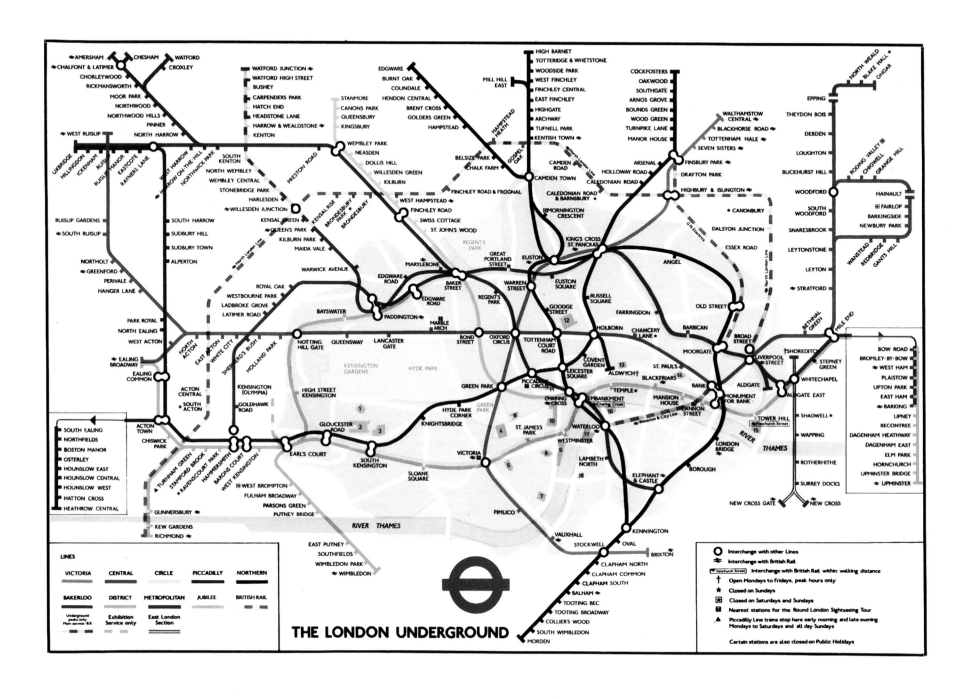

THE LONDON UNDERGROUND

LINES

VICTORIA	CENTRAL	CIRCLE	PICCADILLY	NORTHERN

BAKERLOO	DISTRICT	METROPOLITAN	JUBILEE	BRITISH RAIL

Underground peaks only Main service - B.R.

Exhibition Service only

East London Section

○ Interchange with other Lines

⇌ Interchange with British Rail

[Fenchurch Street] Interchange with British Rail within walking distance

† Open Mondays to Fridays, peak hours only

★ Closed on Sundays

⊞ Closed on Saturdays and Sundays

⊡ Nearest stations for the Round London Sightseeing Tour

▲ Piccadilly Line trains stop here early morning and late evening Mondays to Saturdays and all day Sundays

Certain stations are also closed on Public Holidays

Above: *The Delft University map was published in 1983 and created by a team led by Paul Mijksenaar. This proposed a topographical centre surrounded by compressed schematised suburbs. The intention was a map that would assist people in deciding which option would be better for a particular journey; Underground versus walking.*

Chapter Three

Winds of Change

Below: *Central area of a 1982 official Underground map. Compared with the map on p. 25, the Circle Line has been stretched vertically to make space for the planned Jubilee Line extension to Fenchurch Street that was subsequently abandoned. This configuration dates from 1973 and forms the basis of many of the maps in this chapter. With Paul Mijksenaar advocating a topographically accurate central area, it is ironic that the official map had become even more distorted compared with previous versions.*

S O FAR, THE UNOFFICIAL MAPS in this book comprise an interesting but rare supplement to the history of mapping the Underground. The 1980s continued to be relatively peaceful in terms of alternative designs but in the background commercial and technological events would subsequently cause a deluge.

The decision that had greatest impact came in 1981, when London Transport commenced charging a licence fee for reproducing the map. Previously, it was believed that widespread dissemination of this was valuable marketing for Underground services and therefore the costs of providing artwork to third party publishers were more than made up for by the fares paid by tourists. Any publisher who wished to use an Underground map could do so free of charge. Subsequently, perhaps in conjunction with the rise of London as a tourist destination, the zeitgeist shifted towards a belief that the design was a powerful, internationally-recognised image and that including it in a tourist guide, or similar publication, would boost third party credibility and sales. Therefore, publishers who benefitted from this should pay a fee that reflected it.

Initially, there was resistance from some long-standing customers but the licence fee requirement soon became accepted practice. However, the requirement for payment provided a new motivation for creating an unofficial map, although this would run into copyright issues (but only in the next decade would these be policed effectively). It should also be noted that even if there was no desire to save money by breaching copyright, a publisher in a distant country, such as Japan, might find daunting the prospect of contacting and negotiating with unknown people in an organisation half way across the world.

At the beginning of the 1980s, the only alternative to the official map would be for a publisher to arrange for one to be physically created and photographed. A hand-drawing would not necessarily be needed because a map can be assembled using adhesive tape for the lines, along with stickers for the stations and symbols, and applying transfers (usually Letraset) for the lettering. Despite this, for a large network such as London, some time, effort and design skills would still be needed for a serviceable product to be created.

The technological advances of this decade were to completely transform the design process. The Apple Macintosh computer, introduced in 1984, was intended to be relatively inexpensive and easy to use, designed from the ground up to have powerful graphics capabilities. Crucially, the expectation was that the appearance of a screen image should match a printout, so that a designer could create a piece of work, safe in the knowledge that there should be no subsequent difficulties in realising this. Unfortunately, the first models were not powerful enough and it was not until the expensive colour-capable Macintosh II was introduced in 1987 that the underlying capabilities could be fully realised.

There are two fundamental ways in which a computer can store and implement an image. Bitmapped graphics are specified by individual dots, or pixels. A high-resolution digital photograph will have millions of these, each coded as a particular colour. The problem this presents to map designers is that the computer has no information about

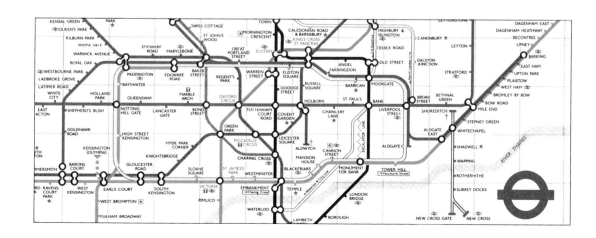

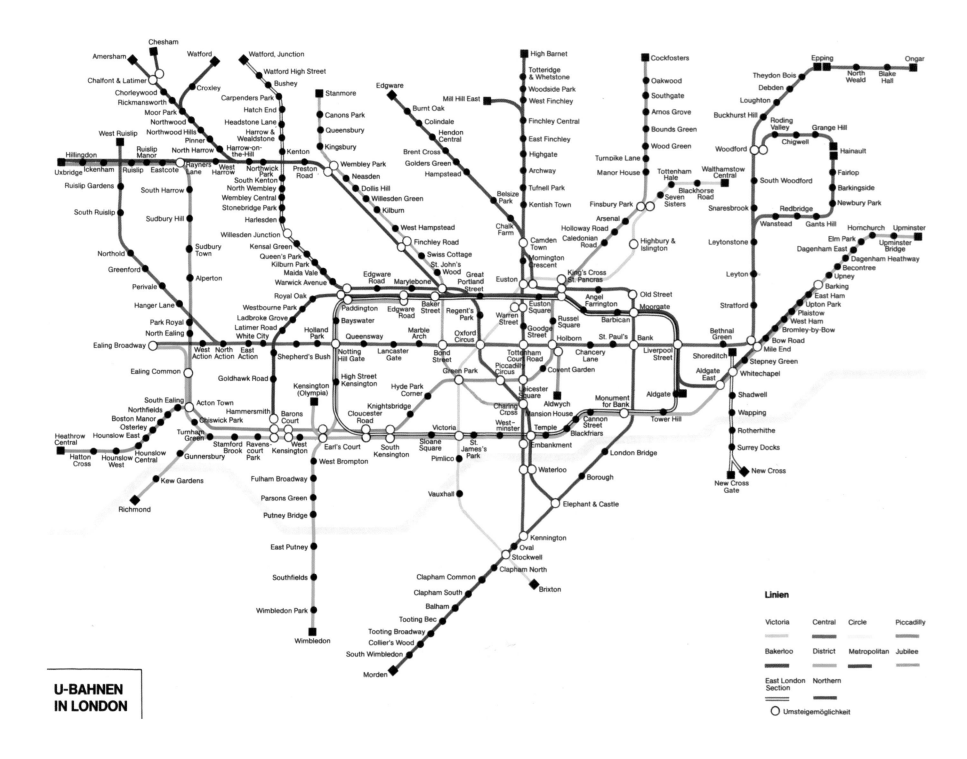

Chesham
Amersham
Watford
Watford, Junction
Watford High Street
Chalfont & Latimer
Bushey
Chorleywood
Croxley
Rickmansworth
Carpenders Park
Edgware
High Barnet
Cockfosters
Epping
Ongar
Moor Park
Hatch End
Stanmore
Totteridge
& Whetstone
Theydon Bois
North
Blake
Weald
Hall
Northwood
Headstone Lane
Burnt Oak
Woodside Park
Debden
Northwood Hills
Harrow &
Wealdstone
Canons Park
Mill Hill East
West Finchley
Oakwood
Loughton
West Ruislip
Pinner
Queensbury
Colindale
Finchley Central
Southgate
Buckhurst Hill
Roding
Grange Hill
Ruislip
North Harrow
Harrow-on-
Kenton
Kingsbury
Hendon
East Finchley
Arnos Grove
Woodford
Valley
Chigwell
Manor
the-Hill
Central
Hillingdon
Rayners
West
Northwick
Preston
Wembley Park
Brent Cross
Highgate
Bounds Green
Walthamstow
Hainault
Ickenham
Lane
Harrow
Park
Road
Neasden
Golders Green
Archway
Wood Green
Turnpike Lane
Tottenham
Central
South Woodford
Fairlop
Uxbridge
Ruislip
Eastcote
South Kenton
Hampstead
Tufnell Park
Hale
Blackhorse
Barkingside
Ruislip Gardens
North Wembley
Dollis Hill
Belsize
Manor House
Seven
Road
Snaresbrook
Newbury Park
Wembley Central
Willesden Green
Park
Kentish Town
Finsbury Park
Sisters
Redbridge
South Harrow
Stonebridge Park
Kilburn
Wanstead
Gants Hill
Harlesden
Arsenal
Leytonstone
Sudbury Hill
West Hampstead
Chalk
Holloway Road
Hornchurch
Upminster
Willesden Junction
Kensal Green
Finchley Road
Farm
Caledonian
Highbury &
Elm Park
Upminster
Northolt
Queen's Park
Swiss Cottage
Camden
Road
Islington
Leyton
Dagenham East
Bridge
Sudbury
Kilburn Park
St. John's
Town
Dagenham Heathway
Greenford
Town
Maida Vale
Wood
Mornington
King's Cross
Becontree
Alperton
Warwick Avenue
Great
Crescent
St. Pancras
Stratford
Upney
Perivale
Royal Oak
Edgware
Portland
Euston
Barking
Hanger Lane
Westbourne Park
Road
Marylebone
Street
Angel
Old Street
East Ham
Park Royal
Ladbroke Grove
Baker
Regent's
Warren
Euston
Farrington
Moorgate
Upton Park
North Ealing
Latimer Road
Paddington
Edgware
Street
Park
Street
Square
Russel
Barbican
Bethnal
Plaistow
Ealing Broadway
White City
Road
Bayswater
Goodge
Square
Green
West Ham
Holland
Oxford
Street
Holborn
St. Paul's
Bank
Liverpool
Bow Road
Bromley-by-Bow
Ealing Common
Park
Queensway
Marble
Circus
Tottenham
Chancery
Street
Mile End
North
East
Notting
Lancaster
Arch
Court Road
Lane
Stepney Green
Goldhawk Road
Action Action Action
Shepherd's Bush
Hill Gate
Gate
Bond
Piccadilly
Shoreditch
Whitechapel
South Ealing
Kensington
Street
Covent Garden
Aldgate
Northfields
Acton Town
(Olympia)
High Street
Hyde Park
Green Park
Circus
Leicester
East
Shadwell
Boston Manor
Hammersmith
Kensington
Corner
Square
Aldgate
Osterley
Chiswick Park
Barons
Knightsbridge
Charing
Aldwych
Monument
Wapping
Heathrow
Hounslow East
Turnham
Court
Gloucester
Cross
for Bank
Tower Hill
Central
Green
Earl's Court
Road
West-
Mansion House
Cannon
Rotherhithe
Stamford
Ravens-
West
Victoria
Temple
Street
Hatton
Hounslow
Brook
court Park
Kensington
St.
minster
Blackfriars
Surrey Docks
Cross
Central
Gunnersbury
West Brompton
South
Sloane
James's
Kensington
Square
Park
Embankment
New Cross
Hounslow
Kew Gardens
Pimlico
London Bridge
New Cross
West
Fulham Broadway
Waterloo
Gate
Richmond
Parsons Green
Vauxhall
Borough
Putney Bridge
Elephant & Castle
East Putney
Kennington
Southfields
Oval
Stockwell
Wimbledon Park
Clapham Common
Clapham North
Clapham South
Brixton
Balham
Wimbledon
Tooting Bec
Tooting Broadway
Collier's Wood
South Wimbledon
Morden

**U-BAHNEN
IN LONDON**

Left and above: After the strange creations of the previous chapter, the German Polyglott Große Reiseführer for London offered a particularly stylish reworking of the official map. It first appeared in 1983, and subsequent revisions added the Heathrow loop and the Docklands Light Railway.

Right: In contrast, the shorter Polyglott Reiseführer continued to offer a monochrome adaptation based on 1960s official maps. This first appeared in 1977, but then inexplicably turned orange in 1984.

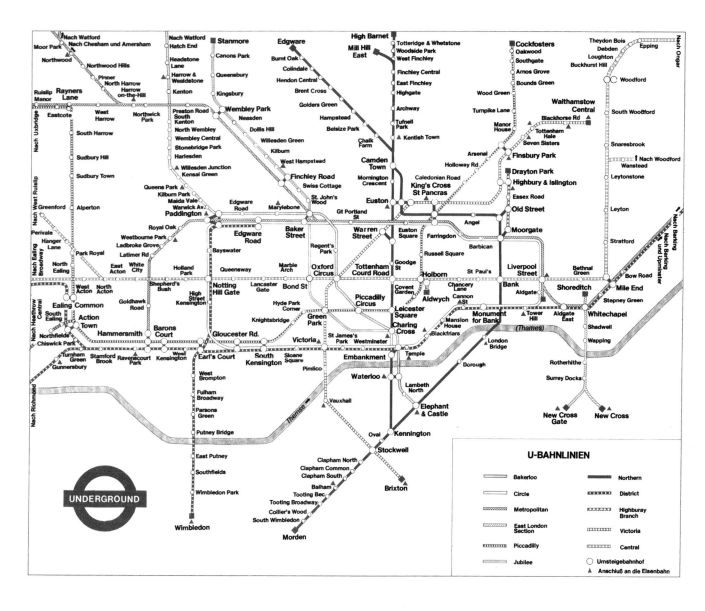

the real-life objects that the dots represent. Hence, the computer cannot determine whether, for example, a black pixel at Stockwell on the Northern Line represents the line itself or else is part of the interchange circle. It is possible to create a bitmapped schematic map but making changes to it is hard work.

Vector graphics are far easier to work with. For these, individual objects, such as a line or an interchange circle, are coded as separate entities in the form of mathematical equations that define their shape (plus information about colour and stroke width). Objects can be placed, copied and modified individually without the computer mixing them up with the others. A vector image can be printed at any size without loss of quality because the equations can be scaled to match the page. For bitmapped images, expanding their size simply makes the dots larger, until individual ones become visible and the image looks grainy (or *pixelated*).

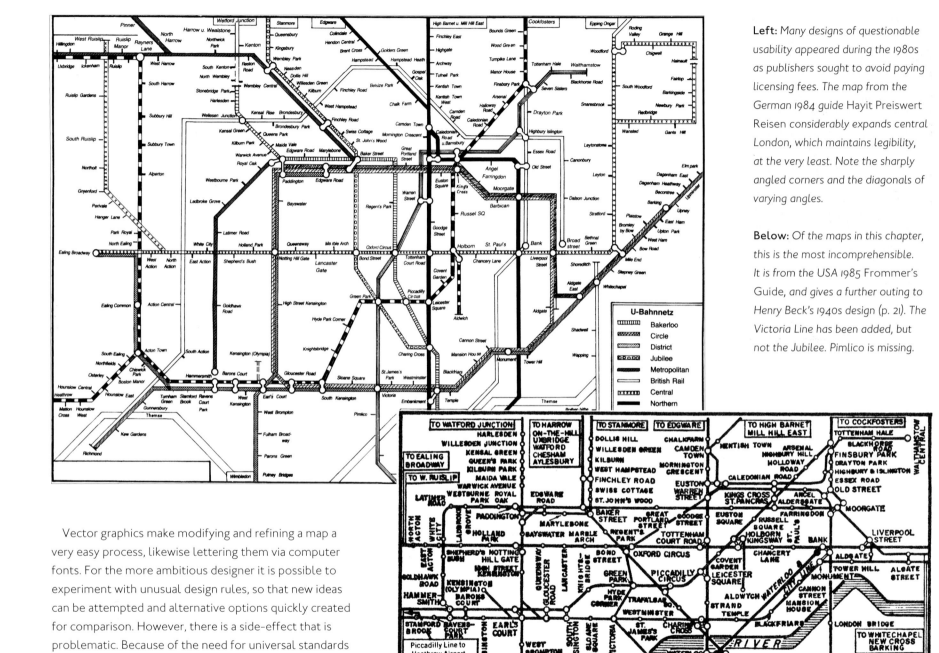

Left: *Many designs of questionable usability appeared during the 1980s as publishers sought to avoid paying licensing fees. The map from the German 1984 guide Hayit Preiswert Reisen considerably expands central London, which maintains legibility, at the very least. Note the sharply angled corners and the diagonals of varying angles.*

Below: *Of the maps in this chapter, this is the most incomprehensible. It is from the USA 1985 Frommer's Guide, and gives a further outing to Henry Beck's 1940s design (p. 21). The Victoria Line has been added, but not the Jubilee. Pimlico is missing.*

U-Bahnnetz

▥	Bakerloo
▨	Circle
▦	District
▣	Jubilee
▩	Metropolitan
▭	British Rail
▥	Central
▬	Northern

Vector graphics make modifying and refining a map a very easy process, likewise lettering them via computer fonts. For the more ambitious designer it is possible to experiment with unusual design rules, so that new ideas can be attempted and alternative options quickly created for comparison. However, there is a side-effect that is problematic. Because of the need for universal standards – so that a map created using a computer in the design studio can be printed by another at the print shop – it can be easy to take a computer file of a map designed by someone else and make changes to it, perhaps in an attempt to disguise the original source. Creators of vector maps guard their intellectual property carefully.

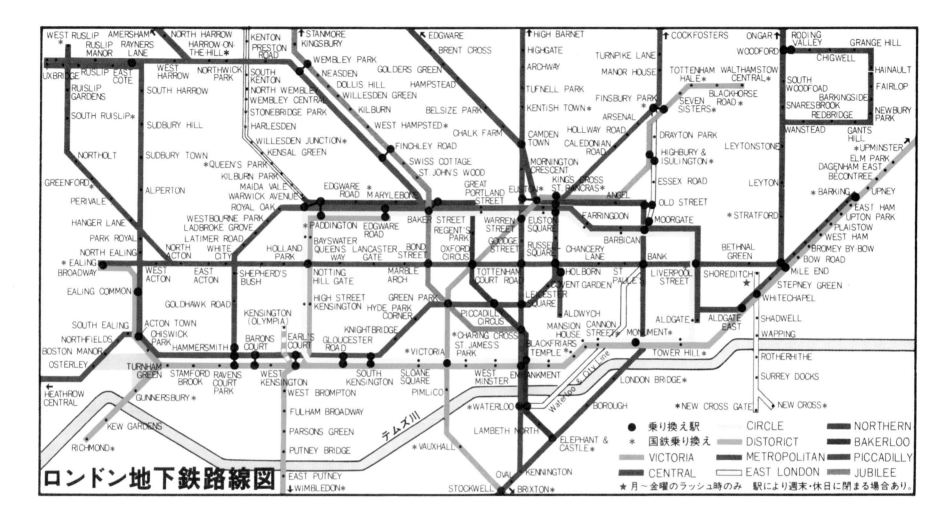

Above: *Many unofficial Underground maps originate from Japan. This one is from the Kadokawa Shoten guide of 1987. Despite the sharp corners and unusual lettering that is often printed on top of the lines, the use of colour at least ensures that these can be followed. Dots for station markers are a frequent international substitution for tick marks. Most puzzling is the giant lake between Gunnersbury and Boston Manor in west London.*

MacDraw was the first vector package for the Macintosh computer, introduced alongside it in 1984. Packages with more features, such as *Adobe Illustrator* (1987) and *Aldus Freehand* (1988), set the stage for designers to create maps of complex urban rail networks, such as the London Underground. Now, a publisher who objected to licensing the official design might be able to obtain a cost-effective alternative instead.

Vector graphics packages provided tools to create high quality digital drawings, such as unofficial Underground maps. Another technological jigsaw piece fuelled some demand for them. Desktop publishing software enabled the assembly of images and text into single publications,

such as a tourist guide, again capitalising on the ability of the Macintosh computer to show the results on the screen as they would appear in print. *Aldus Pagemaker* was first released in 1985, and *Quark Xpress* in 1987. With the latest computer technology, a publisher could now easily produce tourist information guides packed with photographs and maps.

In terms of the unofficial designs from this decade, the most interesting one, perhaps most useful to tourists, ironically never appeared in a guidebook (p. 28). The Delft University map was created as a result of fieldwork in London conducted by designer Paul Mijksenaar and twelve students. This included visits to interchange stations and

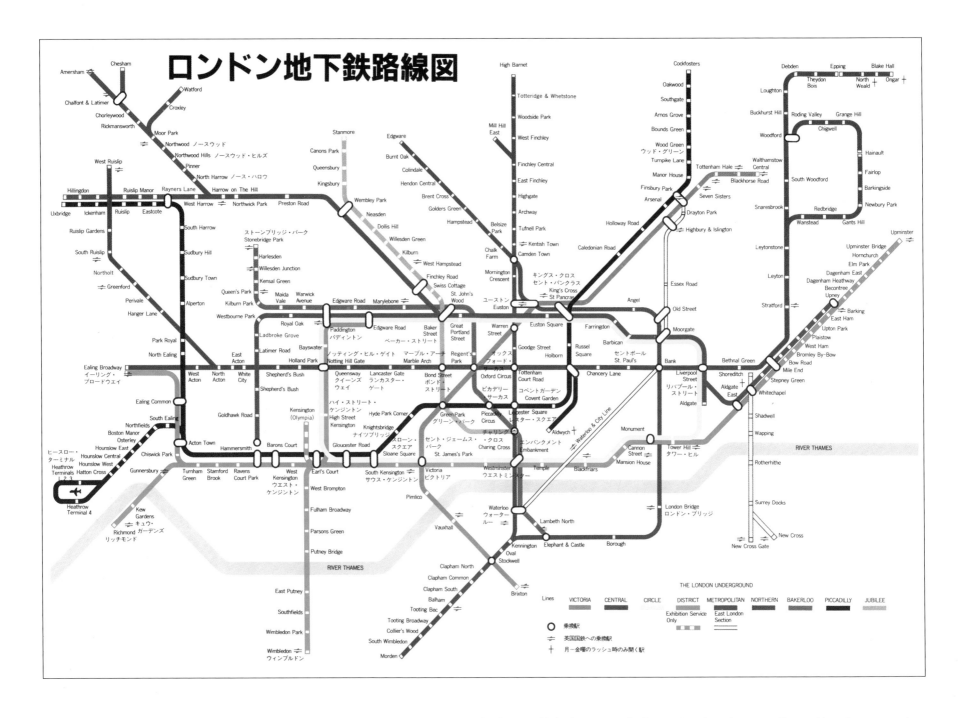

ロンドン地下鉄路線図

Above: *Unlike the Japanese map on p. 33, this design published by KNT in 1987 looks far more professional, and was printed in vibrant spot colours. The base design is the compact diary map produced by London Transport in the 1970s and 1980s. Several suburban stations have been transliterated into Japanese and it is interesting to see which of these were deemed important enough to receive this treatment. Some, such as Wood Green, seem to be surprising choices. [35 by 25 cm]*

Right: *This unauthorised central London design was included on the VistaGuide London map in 1989. Embarrassingly, it was offered for sale at the London Transport Museum. The publisher tried to get around the copyright issue by claiming that it was "Based on the London Transport Underground Map (1936) and amendments derived from original research carried out by Fernando Benito." A comparison with the map on p. 14 shows that this is, indeed, plausible. However, with Henry Beck's death in 1974, the 1936 map would have been just as much protected by copyright as the 1989 official version. The problem for London Transport was that, even by 1989, there was not a well-defined policy on intellectual property and also the copyright status of Beck's early designs was not clear: he had worked on the original in his own time as a personal project and there was no formal paper record of copyright reassignment. Hence, there was a wariness of pursuing the publisher in the event of a defeat that could create an adverse legal precedent, encouraging a deluge of unofficial maps evading licence fees.*

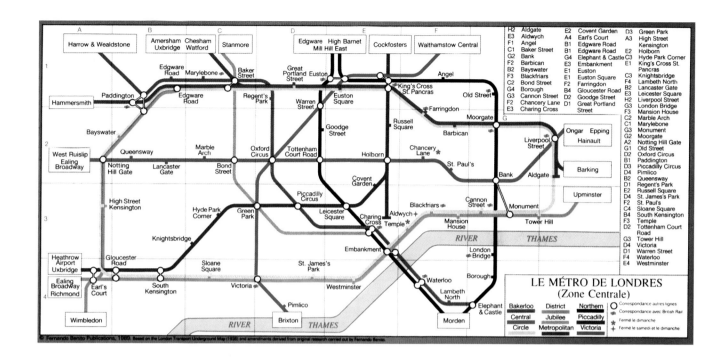

interviews with passengers. Their conclusion was that for many journeys in central London involving one or more interchanges the inconvenience of changing trains often made travel times worse than walking, hence there was a need to help people infer these durations without them having to consult multiple maps. The result was a design in which the clear, colourful, bold Underground lines were maintained but with a topographical central area – which naturally lent itself to the addition of major streets, parks and tourist attractions – and compressed diagrammatic suburbs, where distances between stations were greater and even those journeys that involved interchanges would almost certainly be faster than walking.

For the less innovative maps, changes might have been expected in their appearance owing to new motivations and technology for creating them. In Chapter 2, colour seems to have been a frequent excuse for producing an unofficial design: the official requirement for up to eight spot colours (or else monochrome) was too lavish for many publishers of London tourist guides and maps, who preferred to use their own colours instead. With the rise of

four-colour process printing – in which four basic inks (cyan, magenta, yellow and black) are combined to make all colours – the bizarre results of previous decades became much rarer. The official map itself switched to four-colour process in 1982, meaning that more universally acceptable artwork would be available to licensees, albeit at a price. For publishers who wished to avoid this, cost effective impersonations were now possible in the correct colours.

All the maps in this chapter contain clues to suggest that they were not produced on a computer. This should not be surprising: a publisher seeking to save costs and avoid a licence fee might be unlikely to invest in state-of-the-art computer equipment. The official Underground map itself was not digitised until 1988, and this was using older-generation software (*Bentley Systems Microstation*) that lacked the functionality and ease-of-use that was being developed for newer systems. The benefits of the latest technology were not yet quite cost-effective enough to make a difference, but this was soon to change and yet more developments were on the horizon to encourage the creation of unofficial maps.

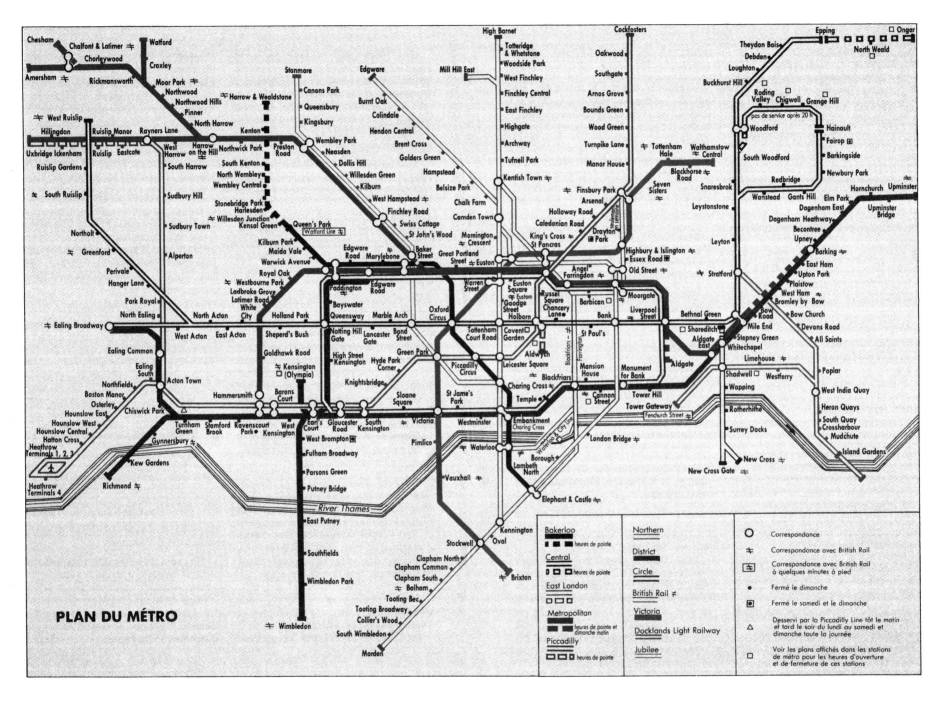

PLAN DU MÉTRO

Above: *French 1990 map from the Guide Arthaud printed in two colours. Despite the date, it is still hand-created. The River Thames has* a strangely wonky trajectory on an otherwise faithful recreation of an official map. Artistic licence has been applied to the British Rail symbols.

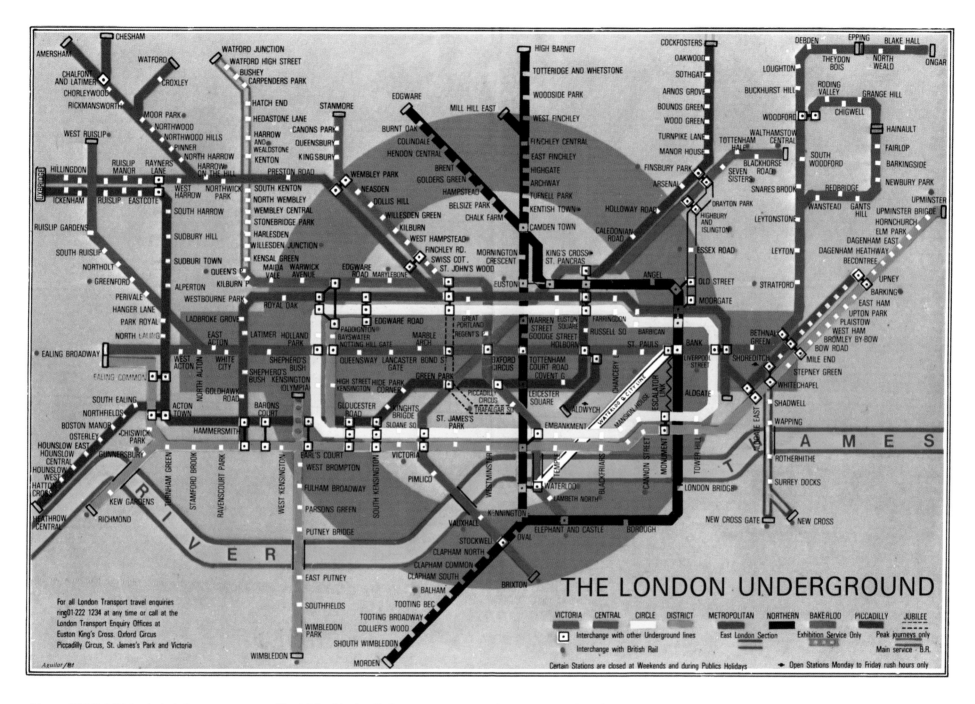

THE LONDON UNDERGROUND

Above: FISA Publishing included this 1990 design in several London tourist guides and street maps. This was based on a 1970s official diary map. The Jubilee Line is still shown as under construction despite being operational since 1979. The thick lines and bitemark stations give the map the appearance of a cubist watercolour painting. The roundel silhouette behind the Circle Line adds neither usability nor credibility.

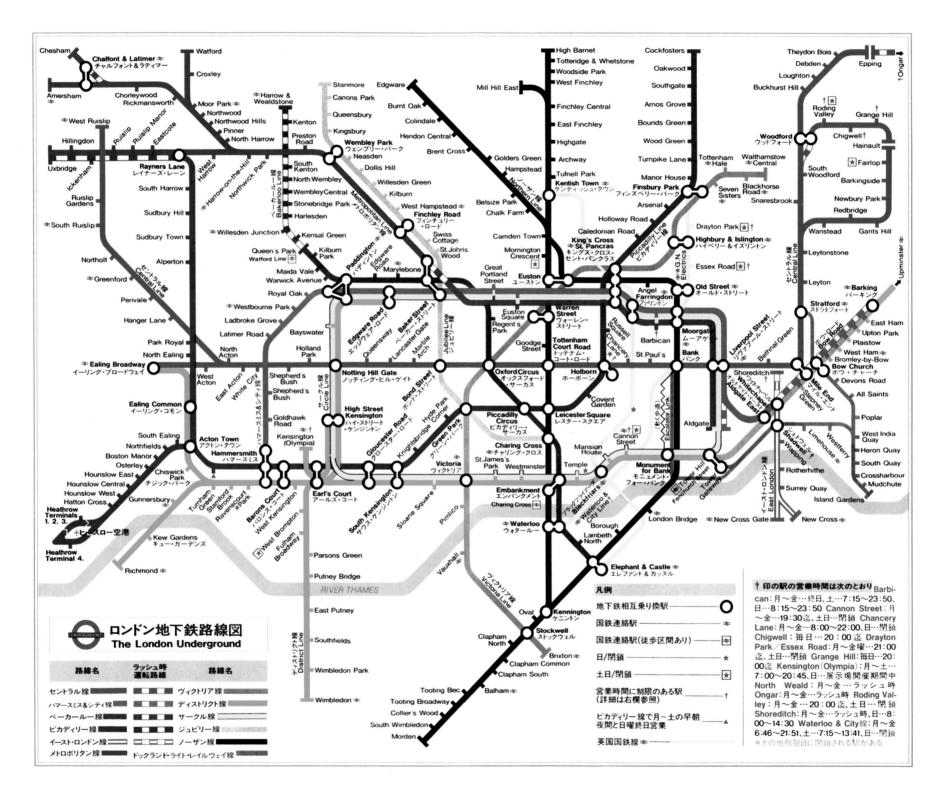

Chapter Four

The Dam Bursts

Left: *The maps in this chapter are in chronological order. Few approach the brazenness of this one from the Japanese 1993 Pack World guide that was published by Jitsugyo No Nihon Sha. Apart from the transliterations and the rotated lettering, only an expert would be able to spot that this was not the real thing. It is also a good candidate for the first computer-produced unofficial map in this book. Pursuing a copyright dispute in Japan would be expensive and require the services of a translator.*

THE 1980s PROVIDED THE TOOLS and motivation for creating unofficial Underground maps but the 1990s created the demand. The demise of Communism in Eastern Europe – symbolised by the dismantling of the Berlin wall (officially commencing in June 1990) heralded new, unprecedented freedom to travel for around three hundred million people.

Airline deregulation legislation had been enacted in the USA in 1978 and was finally implemented Europe-wide in 1987. This ended restrictions as to which operators were permitted on particular routes, enabling new airlines to offer flights and also giving them freedom to set fares. In the wake of this, the rise of budget airlines (Easyjet and Ryanair both began in 1995) provided the means for the new demand to be satisfied cost-effectively, as well as encouraging more travel generally.

All these factors are reflected in the rise of London as a tourist destination. There were around six million visits in 1980 and this increased to seven million in 1985, nine million in 1990, and from 1995 onwards reached a ten year plateau of around twelve to thirteen million per year. In fifteen years the potential market for guides to London almost doubled and powerful computers equipped with desktop publishing packages enabled publishers easily to produce lavishly illustrated books. To include a map of the London Underground would undoubtedly help people plan their visits and, if any publishers did not want to pay licence fees to London Transport, then computer vector graphics provided tools for them to create their own versions in just a few days. It is no exaggeration to say that London Underground map creation became a minor cottage industry in the 1990s.

London Transport needed to respond to unauthorised derivative works but the events of the previous decade had exposed its lack of preparedness. Working parties, and also consultations with legal experts, culminated in 1991 with the publication of an internal brochure: *How to use and protect the intellectual property rights of London Transport*. This described three key intellectual property elements (the roundel, the New Johnston typeface, and the Underground map) and gave an overview of the new

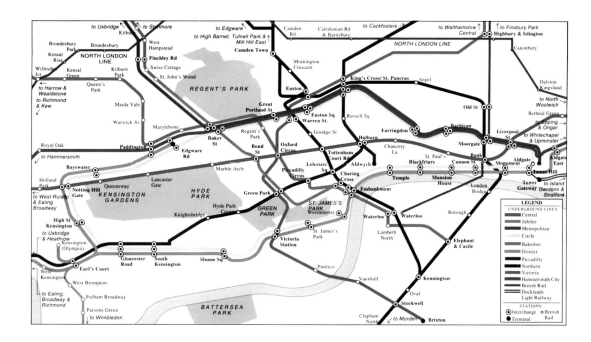

Left: *A tourist guide map need not be a diagram, although this apparently topographical design from the USA 1994 Let's Go guide is somewhat elongated horizontally. Astonishingly, it was targeted in a letter of 20th August 1996 from London Transport in which it was stated that "The map causes us great concern not only from a copyright point of view, but it is also totally misleading". Complaints included the colours of the lines and missing stations, but the suggestion was for an officially licensed design rather than improvements. The allusion to a potential copyright breach is nonsense, but the letter seems to have had the desired effect and an official map was included from 1998 onwards. Of course, with topographical distortion, the official map is famously misleading in its own ways, too.*

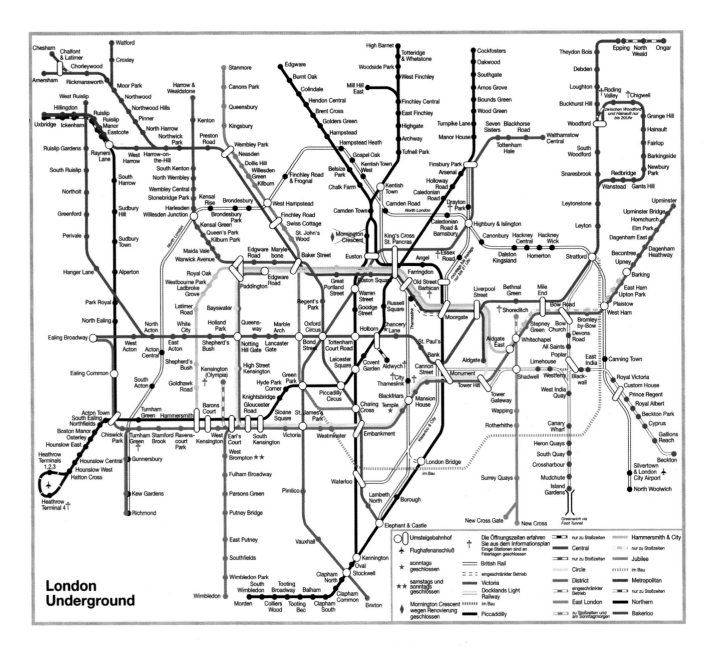

London Underground

Left: *German* Merian *travel guides have been including this design since 1994, making it the longest-lived unofficial map in the book. It has appeared in French- and Spanish-language guides too. The vertical elongation means that the diagonal angle is closer to 55° than 45°. Note the absence of the River Thames.*

Right: *The most recent version of the* Merian *design was published in 2018. Unofficial maps tend to be updated less conscientiously than official ones. Hence the increasing impression of craziness as more and more non-standard angles are added by successive designers in order to accommodate new lines. The Crossrail route in southeast London is particularly deranged and a spurious interchange is shown at Oxford Circus. Unlike official maps,* Merian *guides persisted for many years in showing the useful Thameslink cross-London railway from Farringdon to Blackfriars, but it has recently been deleted. This is ironic considering that enhanced services now run.*

co-ordinated procedures for protecting, licensing, and marketing the use of these. The document also described licensing guidelines and gave an outline of permissible versus non-permissible use. All issues concerning any intellectual property, whether for advice or more concrete proposals, were to be funnelled through a central unit which essentially acted as a clearing-house.

Administratively, this unit was attached to the London Transport Museum, with the licensing revenue being used to support its preservation work. Later, it was subsumed by Transport for London but today protection of intellectual property is out-sourced to a third party.

If there is one negative to the structure that was set in place it is that the same people tasked with defending

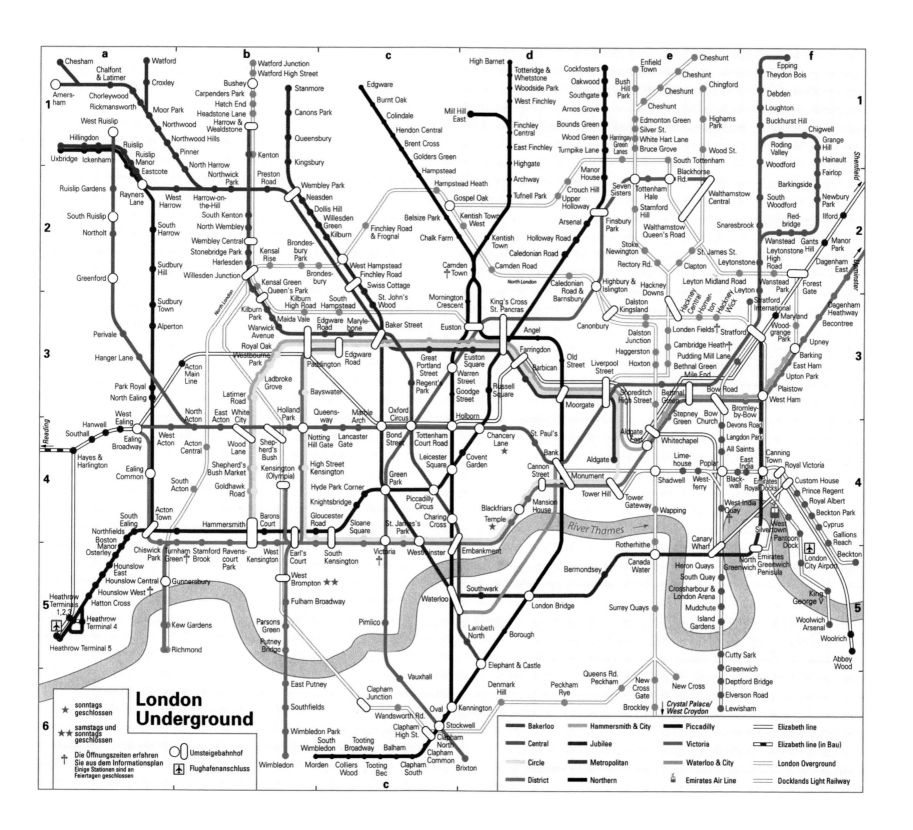

London Underground

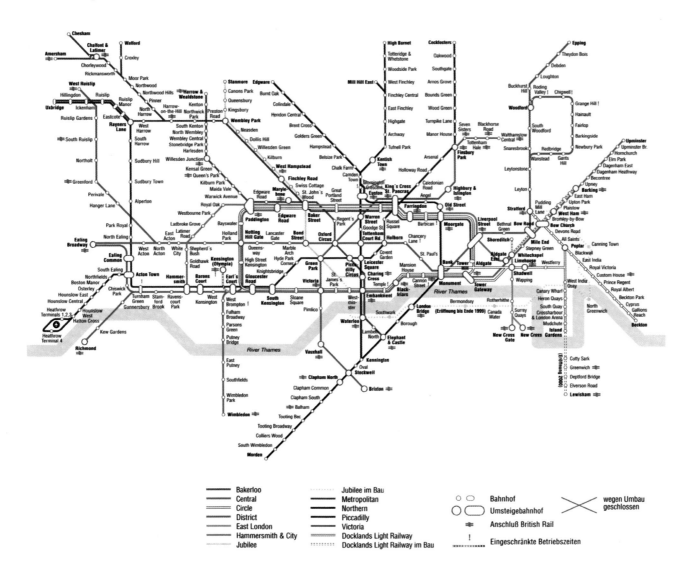

— Bakerloo	···· Jubilee im Bau	∘ ⬭ Bahnhof	✕ wegen Umbau geschlossen
— Central	— Metropolitan	⊝ ⬭ Umsteigebahnhof	
— Circle	— Northern	⇌ Anschluß British Rail	
— District	— Piccadilly		
— East London	— Victoria	! Eingeschränkte Betriebszeiten	
— Hammersmith & City	⫶⫶ Docklands Light Railway		
— Jubilee	⫶⫶ Docklands Light Railway im Bau		

Left: From 1995 onwards, German Polyglott guides replaced the map shown on p. 30 with a new design; the 1999 one shown here is the earliest use, known to the author, of an all-London version. The crooked route taken by the under-construction Jubilee Line extension to Stratford ominously suggests that the designer might not have thought about future-proofing the work.

Right: The Polyglott design continues to this day, as shown by this 2019 version. The ambiguous layout of the Docklands Light Railway near West India Quay has been maintained. The London Overground additions have been achieved more successfully than the Jubilee Line extension but numerous non-standard angles have crept in: Tottenham Court Road is particularly irksome from the perspective of 'good design'. The Heathrow Loop does not show the service pattern clearly. Surely a map in a tourist guide aimed at international travellers should be displaying the correct service to a key UK entry/ exit point?

intellectual property were also those tasked with bringing in licensing revenue. With these two roles combined, it is conceivable that there might have been a natural incentive to overstate the legal position, not only to maximise income for a good cause but also to show to the world the futility of any attempt to map the Underground in any way that might be deemed to tread on the toes of London Transport. There might also have been incentive for guardedness: a public statement that defined exactly what would versus would not constitute a breach of copyright

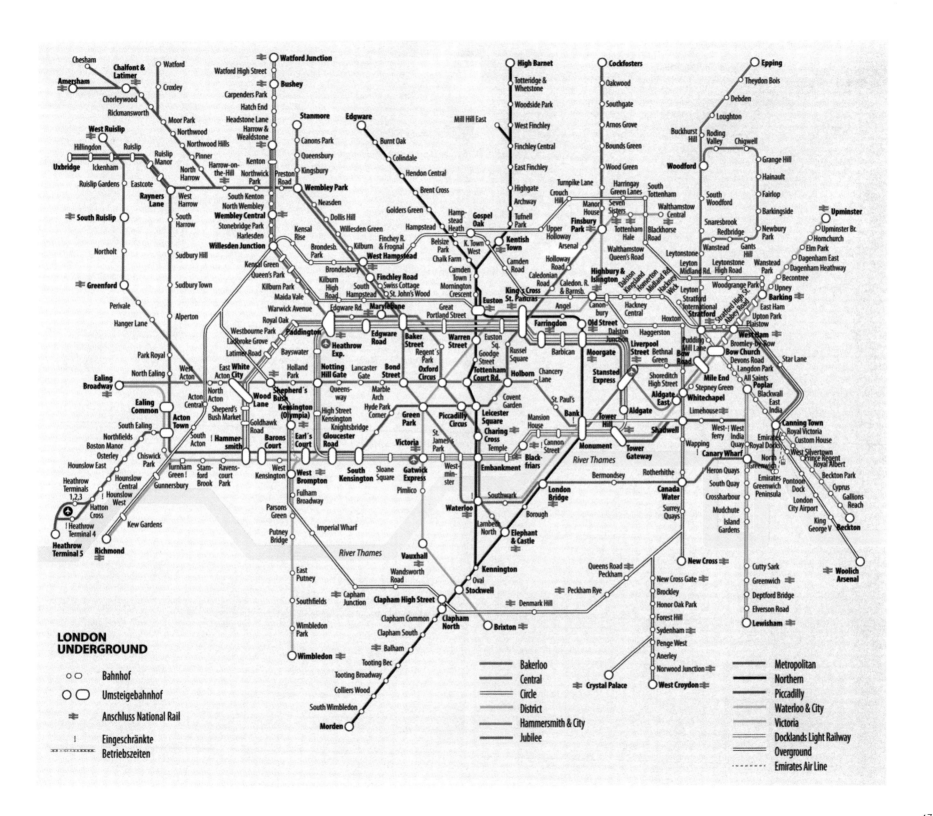

LONDON UNDERGROUND

○ ○	Bahnhof
○ ⬭	Umsteigebahnhof
⇌	Anschluss National Rail
!	Eingeschränkte
	Betriebszeiten

──	Bakerloo	──	Metropolitan
──	Central	──	Northern
──	Circle	──	Piccadilly
──	District	──	Waterloo & City
──	Hammersmith & City	──	Victoria
──	Jubilee	══	Docklands Light Railway
		══	Overground
		┄┄┄	Emirates Air Line

43

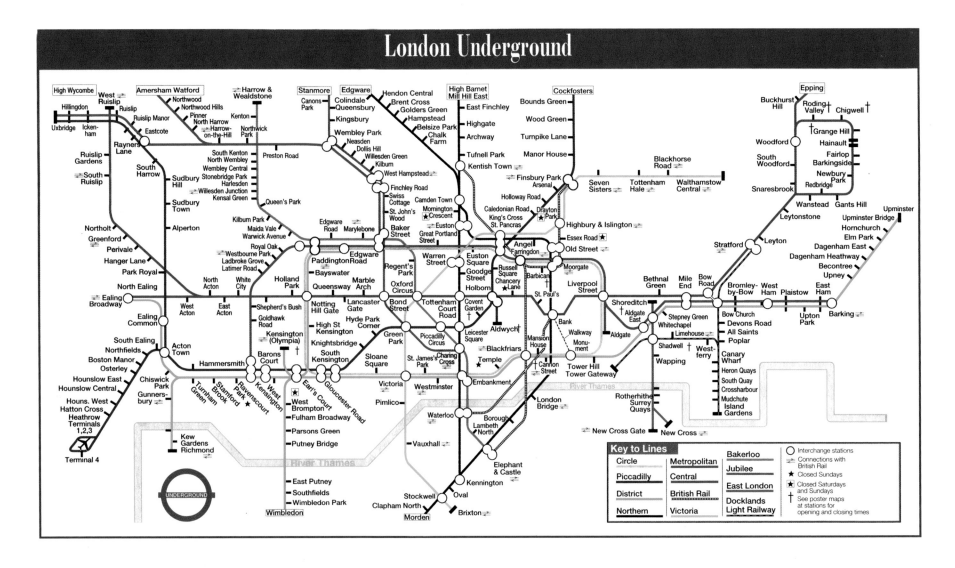

London Underground

could potentially bring down the house, with would-be designers now given precise specifications so that they could safely create legal versions. This is not to suggest that questionable practices ever took place but merely to observe that when people are given incentives to act in certain ways this tends measurably to slant their behaviour. It is also a sad fact that, in a copyright dispute, irrespective of right or wrong, the party most likely to win is the one with the most money and this can also influence the tone with which disputes are pursued. However, the Internet seems to have unleashed unstoppable forces which, at the very least, enable experimental works to be disseminated widely with minimum risk to designers. Today, a simple search will reveal an astonishing array of alternative designs and people can now see for themselves what is possible – but that is to get ahead of the story.

Above: *This map was first seen in 1996, in Frommer's guide:* London from $60 a day. *When its run ended in 2001, $85 per day was required to enjoy London. The map features probably the worst-proportioned roundel ever created. [30 by 17 cm]*

Above right: *Central area of a 1991 official Underground map. Note the bends that have appeared on the* Northern Line around Euston and the Central Line around Bank, compared with previously (p. 29). These were first applied in 1990 and unofficial designs slowly, dutifully followed.

Right: *1999 design from the Austrian Freytag & Berndt folding street map of London. Using black for Bakerloo and Northern Lines and British Rail results in unfortunate confusion.*

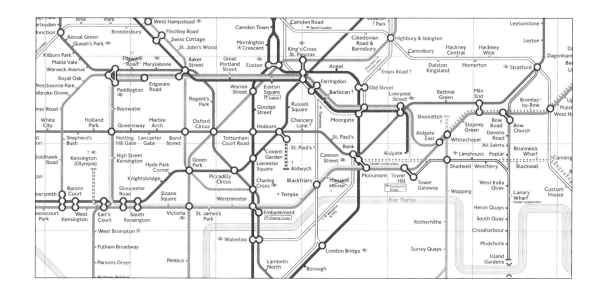

The obvious question – given that a clear intellectual property policy was put in place by London Transport, alongside a robust attitude to its implementation – is *why are there so many maps in this chapter?* There are several reasons for this, not least that, except in very rare cases where a naive publishing company might make contact in advance to seek permission, attempts at enforcement were necessarily reactive, depending on serendipity and/or research. There are travel and foreign language bookshops in London where relevant sections might be scrutinised for offenders (unfortunately, the number of specialist shops has considerably reduced in the last decade) but only approximately one-third of the maps in this chapter were purchased by the author in UK shops.

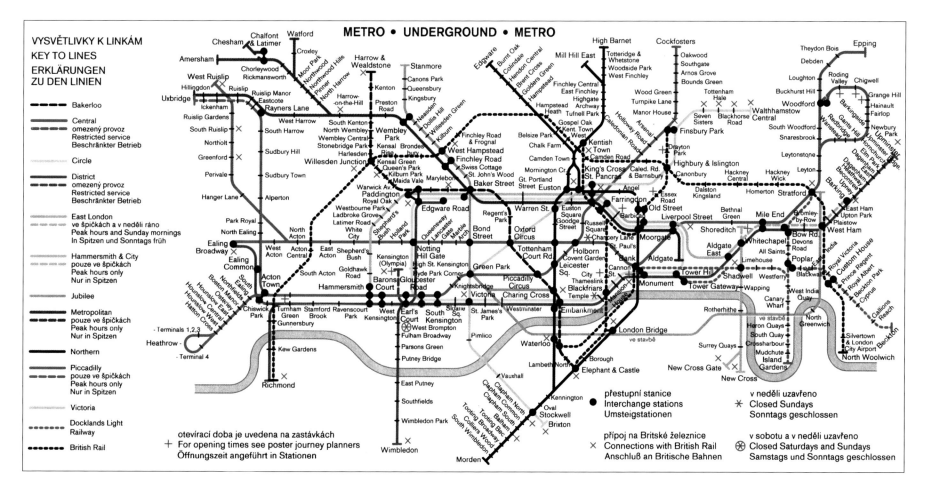

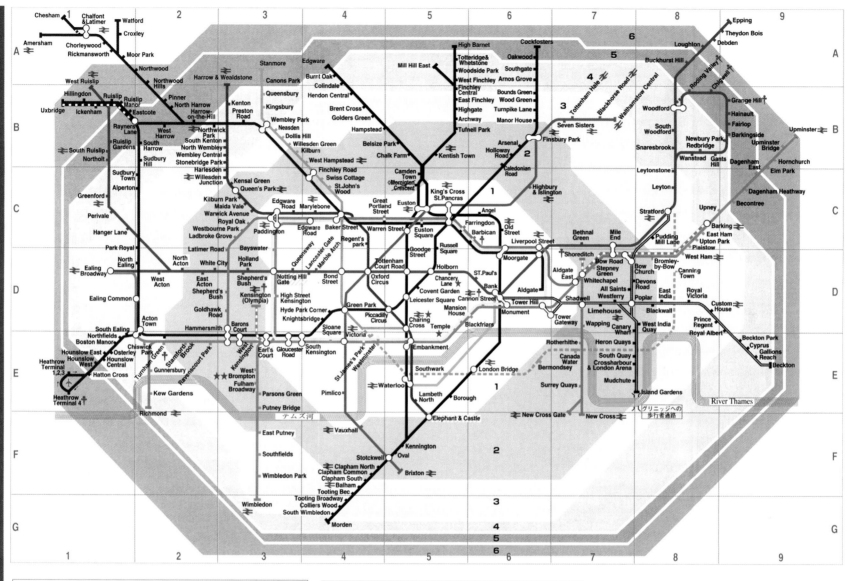

ロンドン地下鉄路線図

Left and right: *Commencing in 1999, another long-lived series. It has appeared in Japanese Globe Trotter guides, published by the Diamond Big Company. The zones are less colourful in the 2019 version but it is clearly the same design. Perhaps adding Crossrail will disrupt its orderliness. [Left: 27 by 21 cm]*

TUBE MAP

ロンドン地下鉄マップ

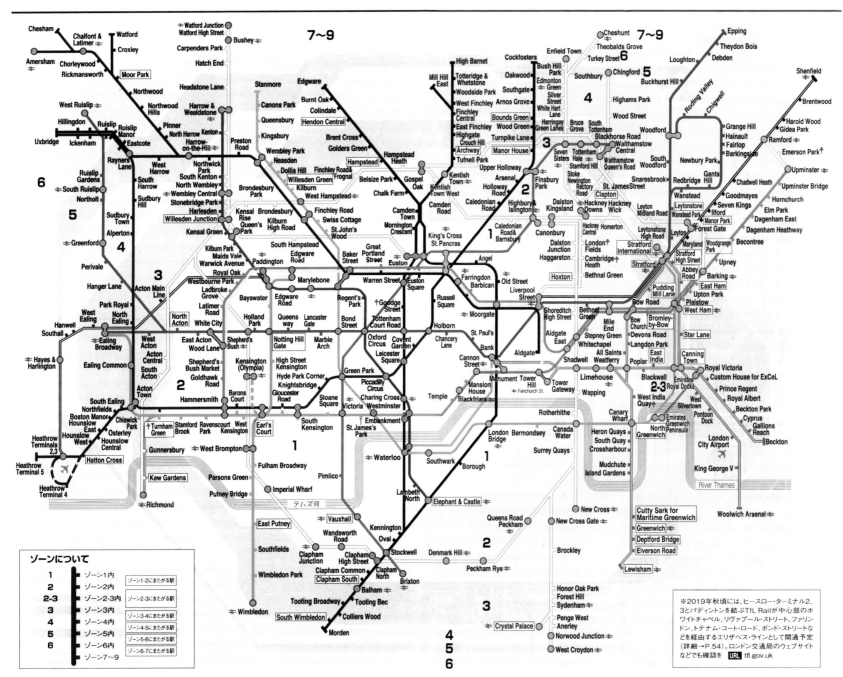

※2019年秋頃には、ヒースロー・ターミナル2、
3とパディントンを結ぶTfL Railが中心部のホ
ワイトチャペル、リヴァプール・ストリート、ファリン
ドン、トテナム・コート・ロード、ボンド・ストリートな
どを経由するエリザベス・ラインとして開通予定
(詳細→P.54)。ロンドン交通局のウェブサイト
などでも確認を URL tfl.gov.uk

47

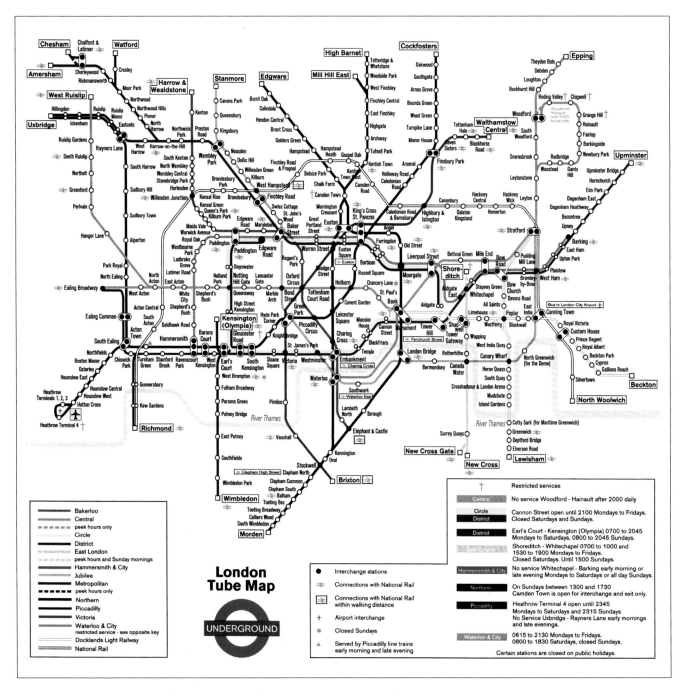

The small unit dedicated to protecting intellectual property, based at the London Transport Museum, simply did not have the resources to travel the world on the off-chance that offending material might be discovered. And, even if derivative works were tracked down, for example in a bookshop in Germany or Japan, the next difficulty would be the time, effort and expense of attempting to instigate an international copyright dispute, compounded

49

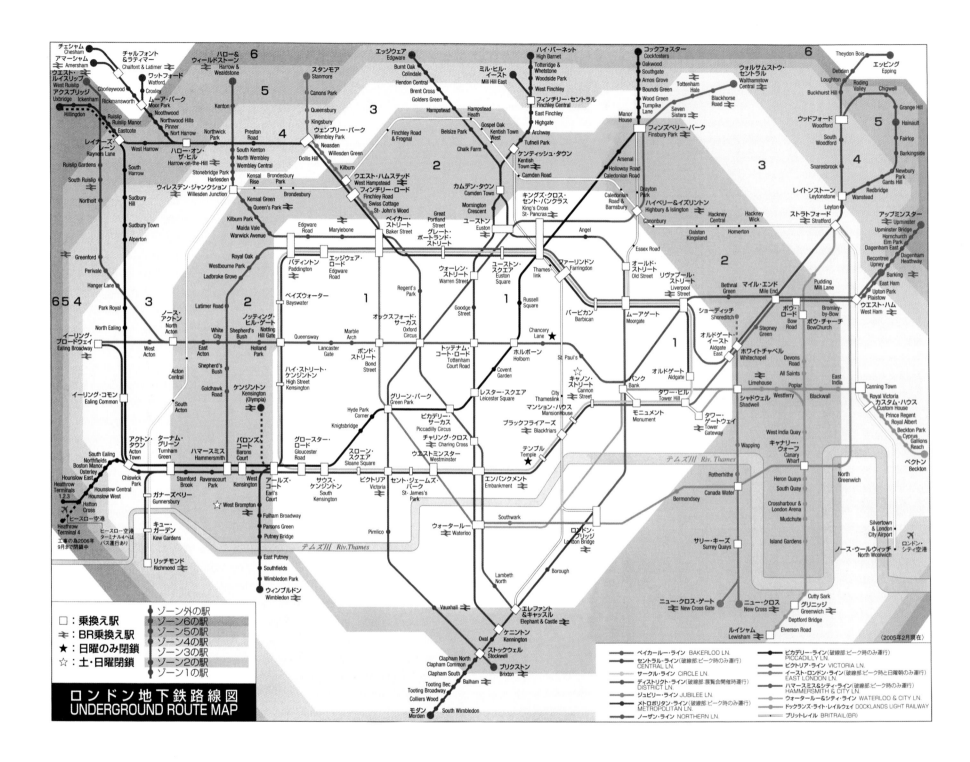

ロンドン地下鉄路線図
UNDERGROUND ROUTE MAP

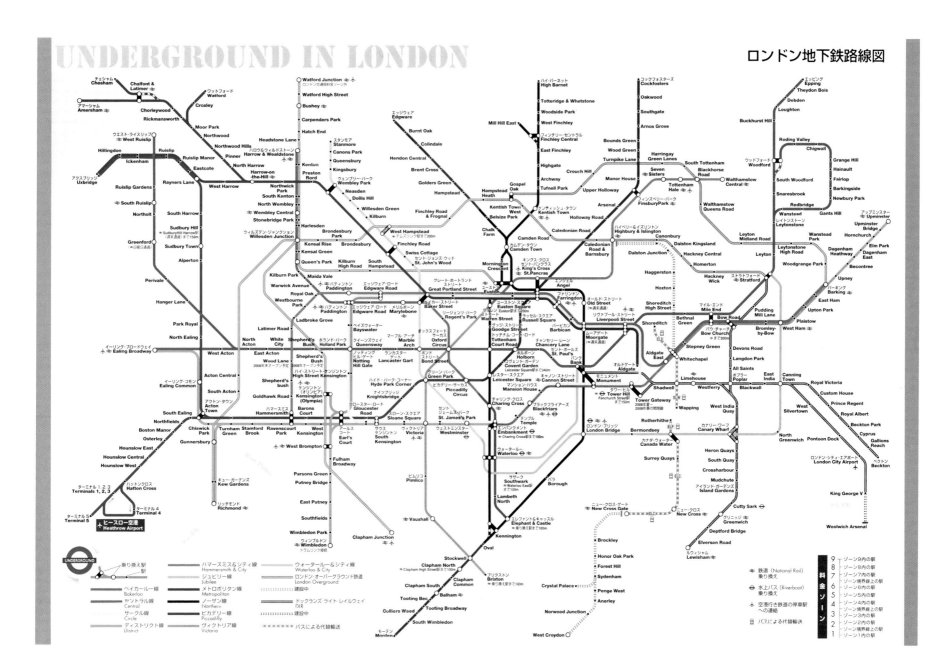

Left: *A colourful map in the 2006 Rurubu guide published by the Japan Tourist Bureau. There might be versions of this from before 2000 judging by the unusual diagonals of the Jubilee Line. The centre is particularly expanded on this design, looking very empty, with distant suburbs pushed into the extremities of the map and looking a bit crushed. [38 by 25 cm]*

Above: *A contrasting map by publisher Shobunsha in the 2009 Mapple guide has a very modern appearance. Japanese maps almost always include fare zones but these are so faintly applied here that they are difficult to see even on the original. The shape of the Heathrow loop correctly implies that the route to Terminals 1,2,3 via Terminal 4 is circuitous. [38 by 25 cm]*

⊕ METRO

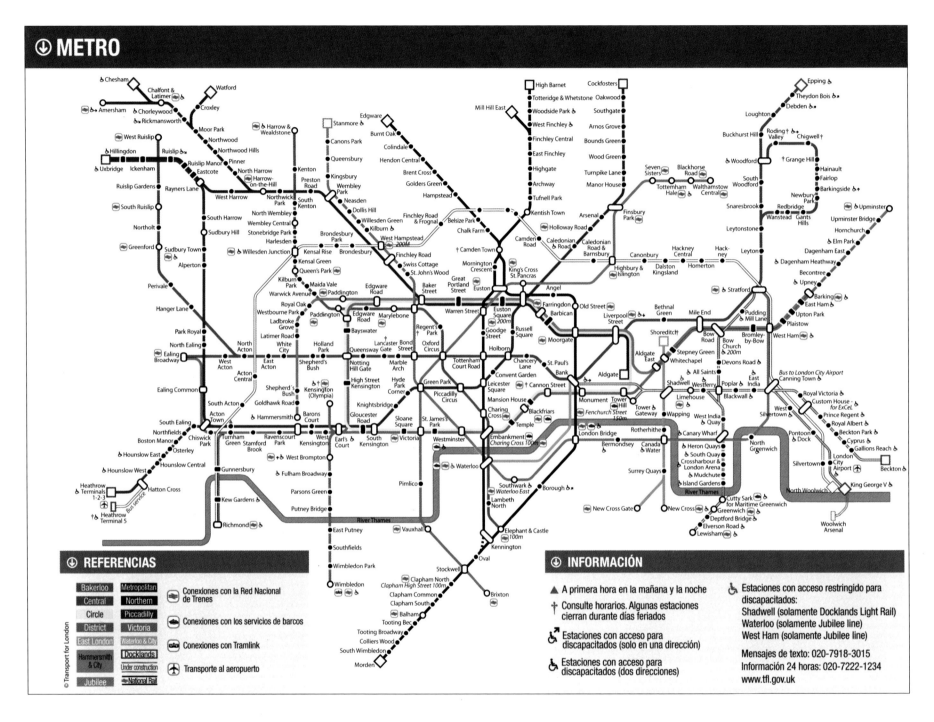

⊕ REFERENCIAS

Bakerloo | Metropolitan
Central | Northern
Circle | Piccadilly
District | Victoria
East London | Waterloo & City
Hammersmith & City | Docklands
| Under construction
Jubilee | National Rail

🚂 Conexiones con la Red Nacional de Trenes

🚢 Conexiones con los servicios de barcos

🚎 Conexiones con Tramlink

✈ Transporte al aeropuerto

⊕ INFORMACIÓN

▲ A primera hora en la mañana y la noche

† Consulte horarios. Algunas estaciones cierran durante días feriados

↗ Estaciones con acceso para discapacitados (solo en una dirección)

♿ Estaciones con acceso para discapacitados (dos direcciones)

♿ Estaciones con acceso restringido para discapacitados:
Shadwell (solamente Docklands Light Rail)
Waterloo (solamente Jubilee line)
West Ham (solamente Jubilee line)

Mensajes de texto: 020-7918-3015
Información 24 horas: 020-7222-1234
www.tfl.gov.uk

by language barriers and differences in cultural attitudes as to how seriously copyright law should be taken. For this reason, the most energy was expended on pursuing

potentially illegal products openly for sale in the UK which covered the major English-language multinational publishers including those based in the USA. This enabled

Left: *2011 design from Argentinian de Dios Editores folding street map of London. Although the configuration is almost identical to the official version, its appearance is subtly altered with large boxes to denote line ends and black dots with white borders for stations. The latter is almost reminiscent of Soviet-style mapping from previous decades.*

Right: *A 2012 map from the Russian Vokrug Sveta guide. Underground stations are denoted by dots and tickmarks, but just dots for the line ends. The Heathrow loop is not configured correctly and Bow Road/ Bow Church stations have obviously caused some confusion. There has been considerable compression to fit the entire network into the space, with the Central Line loop squashed into an unusual shape, and the southern end of the Northern Line is well on the way to Heathrow airport.*

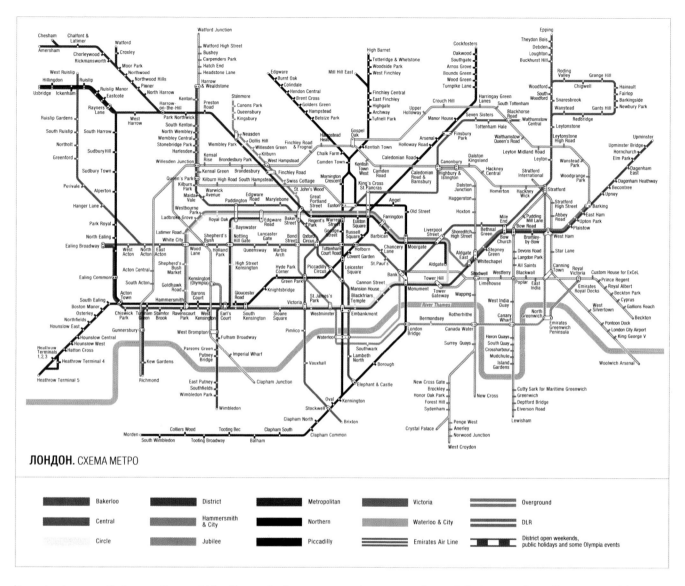

ЛОНДОН. СХЕМА МЕТРО

Bakerloo	District	Metropolitan
Central	Hammersmith & City	Northern
Circle	Jubilee	Piccadilly

Victoria	Overground
Waterloo & City	DLR
Emirates Air Line	District open weekends, public holidays and some Olympia events

licensing income that more than paid for the cost of enforcement, ensured a sufficiently high profile for the unit to act as a deterrent and prevented the potential embarrassment of derivative works being offered for sale at the London Transport Museum. Irrespective of these benefits, action against genuine offenders is essential. The holder of intellectual property must attempt to defend it from misuse, or else risk losing legal protection for it.

Can any trends be identified from all these maps, and the others in the author's collection? In simple terms, the largest numbers of designs are from Germany and Japan, with Italy and France together sharing a distant third place. Serial offenders – designs which have been maintained for many years, or even decades, are only known to the author for Germany and Japan; the rest are one-offs, or only last a few years before being replaced – not necessarily with an official version. These observations are not surprising: Japan and Germany are populous countries, and Germany also has a tradition for international travel. The USA might seem under-represented given its size but, as users of the

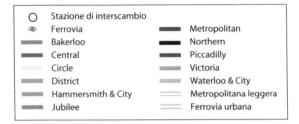

METROPOLITANA

UNDERGROUND

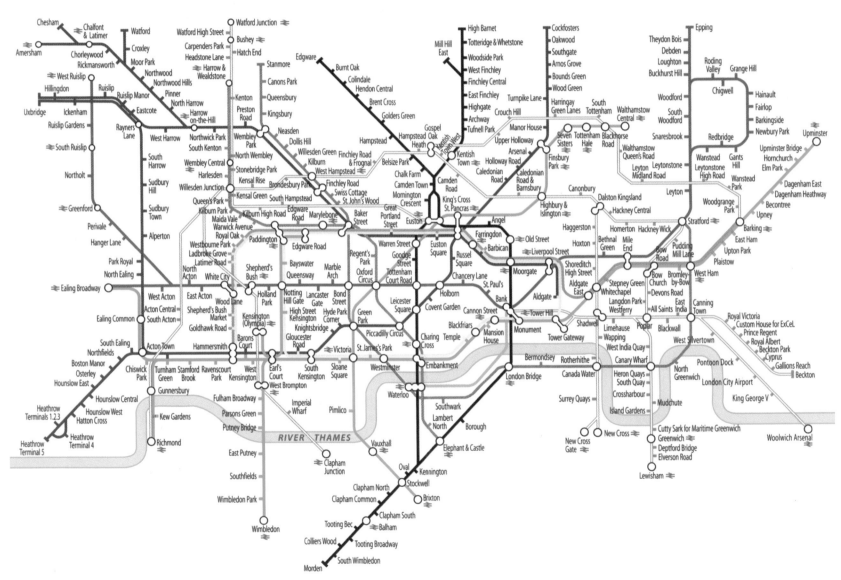

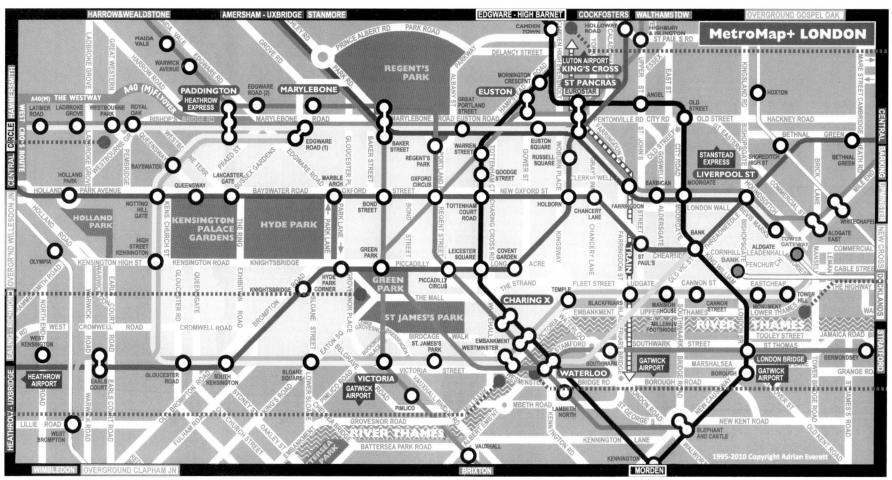

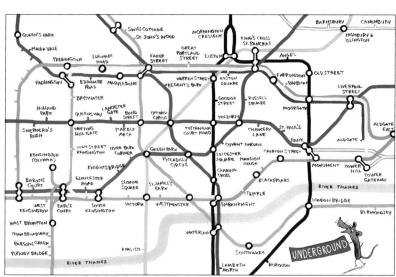

Left: *2012 map from the Italian Giunti guide. The sharp corners and random angles are not a good advertisement for the designer.*

Above: *If the Underground map distorts the topography of London, then why not change the layout of the major streets to match. Research does suggest that experience with the Underground map affects*

people's understanding of the shape of London and this 2012 British Go Metro map cleverly takes this to its logical conclusion. [27 by 14 cm]

Right: *Another Italian map, this time a charming hand-drawn version from the 2015 Le Guidine Londra, published by Edizione EL. Rodents are often seen on the Underground so the logo is strangely appropriate.*

Metro
w Londynie

○ stacja z możliwością przesiadki

Bakerloo
Central
Circle
District
Waterloo & City
Hammersmith & City
Jubilee
Metropolitan
Northern
Piccadilly
Victoria
DOCKLANDS
National Rail

Left: *This 2015 map from the Polish Pascal guidebook is surprisingly clean and clear. One reason for this might be that Overground services are shown using black pecked lines: too much orange can be overbearing. However, there are a number of mistakes. For example, Edgware Road is shown as a single station and the Hammersmith & City Line calls incorrectly at Aldgate. Bow Road and Dalston Kingsland have also caused some confusion.*

Right: *French-Canadian guidebook, Escale à Londres, published by Ulysse in 2016. Blobs are used to denote stations, very much in the style of the current Paris Metro Map. Despite this, the origins of this version are clear: the bends in the Central Line at Marble Arch show that the online version of the official map was the inspiration, which has a slightly different configuration to the printed pocket version. In east London the casing has not been layered properly, giving some strange effects where lines cross.*

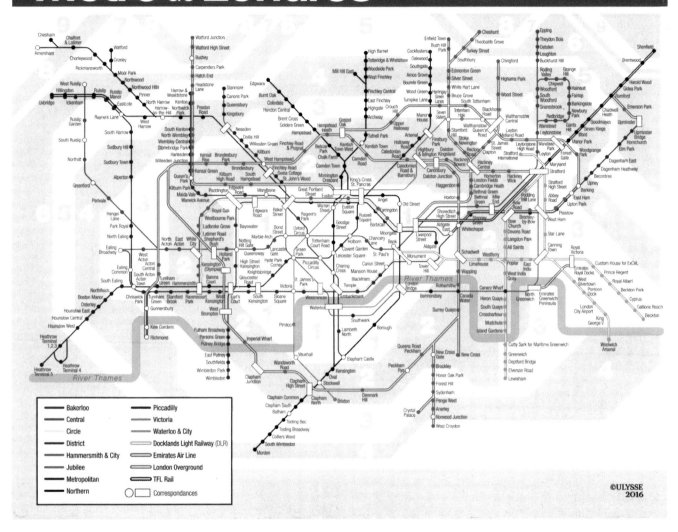

Métro de Londres

English language in a country with a punitive legal culture, reputable publishers are easy targets for the protectors of Underground intellectual property. Also, the American tourist guide market is dominated by a few big names. In general, large multinational publishers, with the exception of German ones, tend to licence official maps: unofficial ones tend to be the found in books published by smaller companies without significant international presence. With determination, unofficial USA maps can be tracked down.

Just counting numbers of maps is simplistic and it is important to consider national preferences, too. London is expensive and, therefore, is not universally popular. Browsing the travel sections of overseas bookshops, it can be inferred that the French would rather visit other parts of France than London and that Spaniards would rather visit South America. Hence, countries with fewer guidebooks published will yield fewer interesting maps. Population and wealth of countries is another factor that

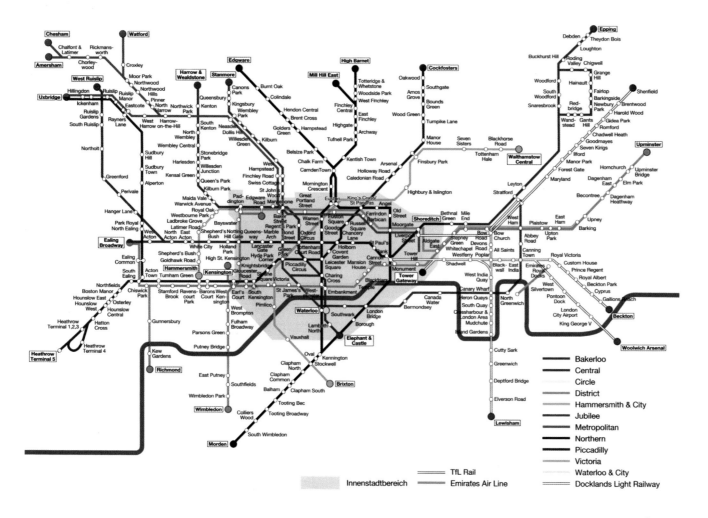

▬▬▬	Bakerloo
▬▬▬	Central
▬▬▬	Circle
▬▬▬	District
▬▬▬	Hammersmith & City
▬▬▬	Jubilee
▬▬▬	Metropolitan
▬▬▬	Northern
▬▬▬	Piccadilly
▬▬▬	Victoria
▬▬▬	Waterloo & City
▭▭▭	Docklands Light Railway

Innenstadtbereich   ═══ TfL Rail   ═══ Emirates Air Line

U-Bahn in London

Left: *The 2017 German Michael Müller guide eschews the London Overground, giving it a very sparse appearance. Unfortunately, advantage was not taken of the space and central London is very cramped. In readiness for the Crossrail opening, the Shenfield suburban service is included but with a spurious interchange at Bow Church. Mysteriously, Aldgate Station and the entire Waterloo & City Line are missing, and the Jubilee Line is shown as still serving Charing Cross: its diversion to Stratford was in 2000.*

Right: *2017 design from the German Borch folding street map of London. The sharp corners, station names interrupting lines and ambiguous junctions all spoil the professionalism of the map.*

has direct implications for travel and guidebook demand, and where opportunities for international travel have only developed relatively recently, multinational publishers have tended to move in quickly to capture the market for travel guides resulting in mainly official Underground maps on shop bookshelves.

Perhaps most interesting of all are the differences in design preferences between countries. For example, Japanese maps almost always show Underground fare zones and German maps rarely do. Perhaps the alien-ness of western culture to the Japanese means that there is a strong desire to have comprehensive travel information in advance, all in one guidebook. Also striking is that French unofficial maps tend to be only very thinly-disguised copies of official versions. German derivative works are far more likely to be better camouflaged. Whether this reflects French disdain for legality or Germanic guilt at breaking the rules is open to debate.

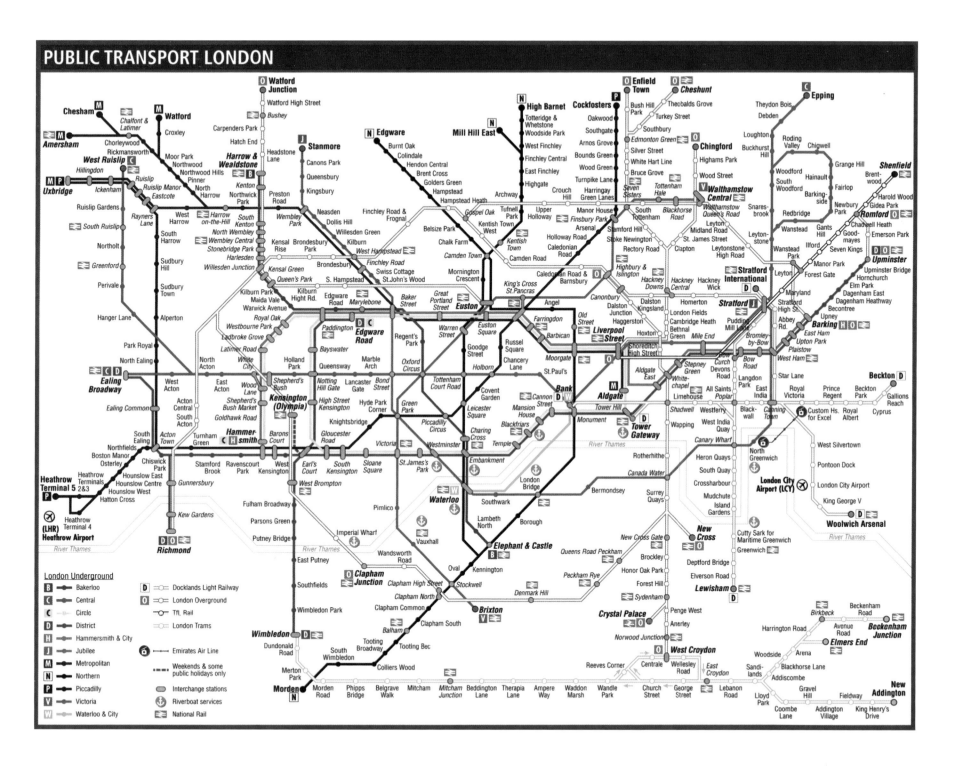

PUBLIC TRANSPORT LONDON

London Underground

B	Bakerloo	D	Docklands Light Railway	
C	Central	O	London Overground	
C	Circle		TfL Rail	
D	District		London Trams	
H	Hammersmith & City			
J	Jubilee		Emirates Air Line	
M	Metropolitan		Weekends & some public holidays only	
N	Northern		Interchange stations	
P	Piccadilly		Riverboat services	
V	Victoria		National Rail	
W	Waterloo & City			

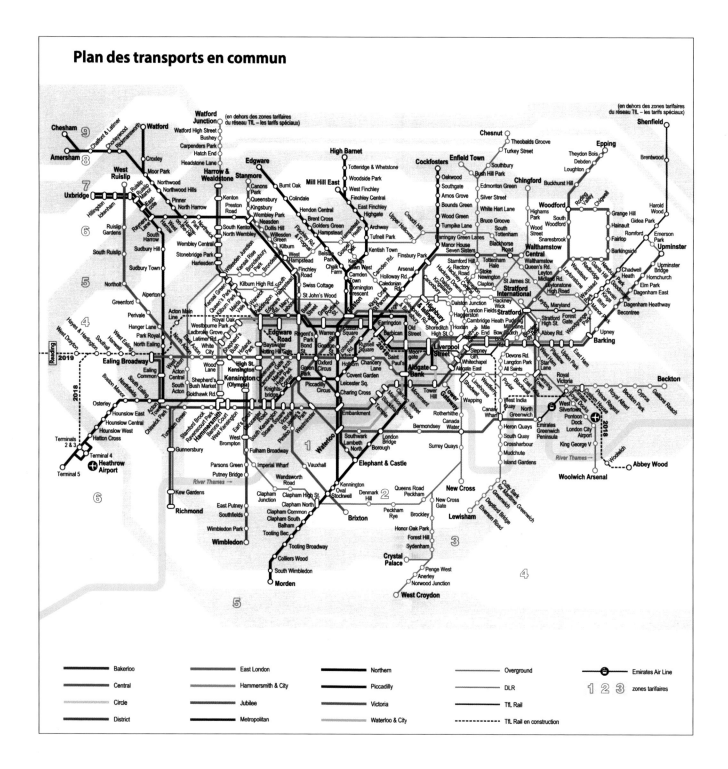

Plan des transports en commun

Left: *Lines too far! The 2017
ExpressMap guide, in French but
published by a Polish company,
presents the traveller with mayhem,
including tightly packed lines and
text rotated in every possible
direction. Crossrail is shown as under
construction but once this opens its
complex interchanges could well
push this map to breaking point.
There are no obvious mistakes but
users will easily make their own,
especially with ambiguous junctions
such as Earl's Court, where there are
no spatial clues as to traffic flow.*

Right: *Despite similar size and
coverage, this Underground map in
the 2018 Dutch mo'media guide is
less of a shambles. Unfortunately,
Crossrail is shown as operational in
readiness for the missed December
2018 target.*

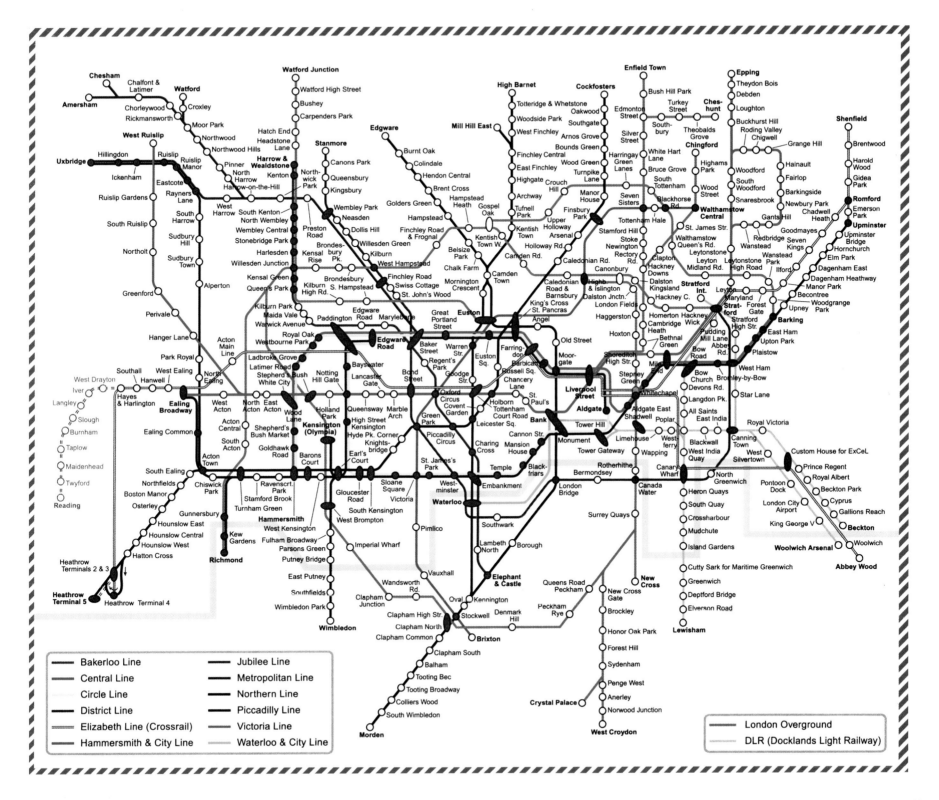

Bakerloo Line
Central Line
Circle Line
District Line
Elizabeth Line (Crossrail)
Hammersmith & City Line
Jubilee Line
Metropolitan Line
Northern Line
Piccadilly Line
Victoria Line
Waterloo & City Line

London Overground
DLR (Docklands Light Railway)

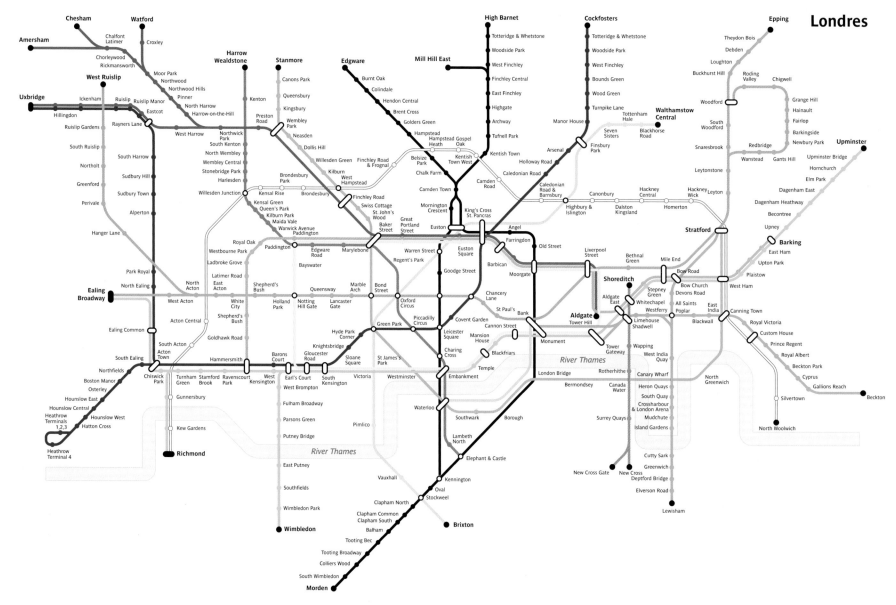

Londres

Chapter Five

Creativity or Camouflage?

Left: *In the early 2000s, the Paris Transport Authority (RATP) website displayed an unofficial map of the London Underground. It used their corporate Parisine typeface, blobs for stations, interchange lozenges, and pastel colours, and was very much in the style of contemporary Paris Metro maps. It is very easy to change the surface parameters of a map and transform its ambience but this cannot hide the fact that it might be a derivative work: for the RATP version there are hallmarks of the official Underground map stamped all over it. The original was only available as a low-resolution jpeg file, the high-res image has been faithfully recreated by the author.*

Below: *Central section of the official Underground map from 2000, the basis for many of the designs discussed in this chapter (see also p. 45).*

IN CHAPTER 4, THE PARENTAGE of almost all of the maps was obvious. Hence, each of these was derivative of an official Underground map but with interesting twists that made them distinctive or unusual. Even so, it was clear that much of the hard work of creating them had actually been undertaken by the design studios commissioned by Transport for London (and its predecessors).

Very occasionally, unofficial maps surface that look dramatically different from official versions, sometimes shockingly so. Clearly the network is being shown in an unusual or unexpected way, leading to the key question: *has the designer demonstrated creativity?* or (for those people who protect TfL intellectual property) *has the designer demonstrated* **sufficient** *creativity for this not to be a work that is derivative of an official map?*

The concept of copyright is subtle and difficult to pin down in terms of absolutes. The key ideas relevant here are *passing off* and *misappropriation*. *Passing off* is effectively a form of counterfeiting, so that a product is falsely represented as being the work of another person or organisation. Hence, creating an unofficial map and applying the Underground roundel to it – as per several examples in these pages – would effectively be attempting to pass it off as an officially sanctioned product, even if this was not the intention of the person adding it to a map.

Misappropriation refers to the *inappropriate use of the ideas, property or work of other people.* But exactly what aspects of these are protected? Mere facts are not ideas or property and are not subject to copyright. Hence, it is a mere fact that there exist railway stations in London, with particular names, that are served in a set order by trains, with opportunities at certain stations to change between these. Anyone can create a map of the London Underground network. It is not possible to prevent that.

The visual appearance of a genre of designs, as defined by the combination of elements that makes them up – the so-called look-and-feel – is notoriously, extraordinarily difficult to protect, as designers of computer interfaces will testify. Hence, a famous type of map might use a particular font, lines at certain widths, in certain colours, at specific angles, and with particular symbols to denote stations and interchanges, but that by itself does not prevent other people from creating maps using the same basic building blocks *even for the same city,* provided that there is no issue with passing off. Look-and-feel only has a strong chance of protection if any of the elements are sufficiently original by themselves to be subject to copyright. In situations such as these it is therefore (some of the) individual elements that cannot be appropriated by other parties, rather than any unique combination of them. Hence, Disney cannot stop other film makers from making *Snow White and the Seven Dwarves* provided that the script is not derivative but it can prevent the lead character from visually resembling its own Snow White. No diagrammatic Underground map has ever utilised a key graphic element that has not previously been used on other designs. The exception is the New Johnston typeface, whose availability is restricted, and there are laws to prevent font extraction and use from, for example, a PDF file. But with Edward Johnston's death in November 1944 his work is now well and truly out of copyright. Anyone may trace his *original* lettering and create a digital font from it.

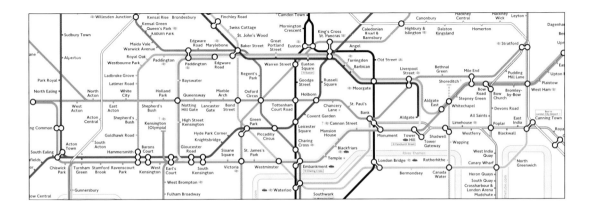

General ideas and concepts also cannot be copyrighted. If Henry Beck had invented any schematisation techniques it might have been possible to patent these, and hence prevent other designers from making use of them, but he did not. In any case, the first whole-network schematised map to use octolinear angles (horizontal, vertical and 45° diagonals) – the most distinctive aspect of his design – was published in Berlin in 1931, two years before Beck's own work was issued. Trademarking likewise cannot assist: this is intended for a simple logo rather than the intricate complexity of an urban rail map. However, the individual elements of a design might be trademarked. Hence, the New York City Subway has protected the colour-letter/colour-number combinations (using the Helvetica font) for the bullets that designate its lines. Restaurants and cafés which display these are pursued accordingly.

What then, exactly, in the context of railway maps, is protected by copyright? The key creative input of the designer is configuring the lines and it is this that will make a genuinely independently produced map unique. This, therefore, should be the focus in resolving a dispute. Official Underground maps have many distinctive aspects to their layouts and unofficial ones that replicate these will be subject to scrutiny. However, configural issues become more complex once it is accepted that certain layouts might comprise *natural solutions*. As any designer will testify, from experience of creating schematic maps, the limitations of applying design rules strictly mean that, in many cases, only certain solutions are feasible. In other words, if a designer starts with a geographical map for reference, selects octolinear angles and adopts sensible design priorities, such as simplifying line trajectories without excessively distorting topography, then it is likely that certain parts of the map will resemble the official version *even if the designer has never seen this before*.

Copyright does not protect a design from such *configural convergence*, only from misappropriation: there has to be a *causal connection* from the original to the disputed work. A *registered design* should be safer from this. Registration prevents an accidental recreation, even if a person has

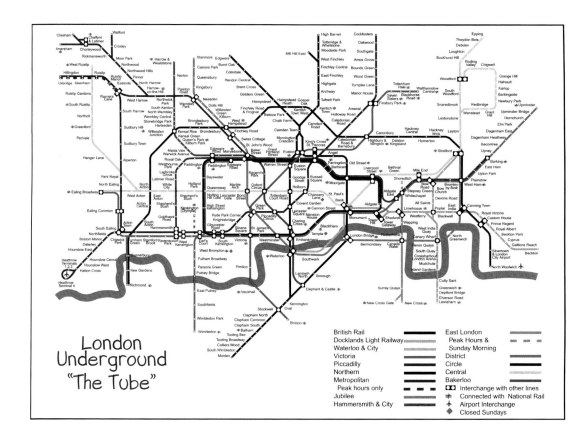

London Underground "The Tube"

no awareness of, or makes no reference to, the original. However, entire genres cannot be registered, only specific designs or else components of them, and the requirement is that these must be original. It is far too late to register Beck's original work, and any elements of later maps that are derivative of his original likewise cannot be registered.

Configural convergence notwithstanding, there are aspects of map design which are less constrained and more open to designer input. The most famous example of this is the so-called *thermos-flask* (or bottle) shape that the Circle Line has been given since 1963. Aspiring Underground map creators who do not want to attract the wrong sort of attention would be advised to focus their creativity here. Other distinctive aspects of the current, official map which are hard to argue as being natural solutions, are the Central Line dive-down from Holborn to Bank and then back up to Liverpool Street, and also the

Above: *The design included in the USA 2002 MapEasy folding street map of London has the interchange circles changed to squares and the station tickmarks to dots. However, the most dramatic alteration is that each line has been recoloured – except the East London, Waterloo & City, and Northern Lines – which certainly transforms the visual impression that it gives. Despite this, every single line bends in the same way, at the same place, as for official maps of the time. Not even the wavy River Thames can detract from the otherwise identically configured design.*

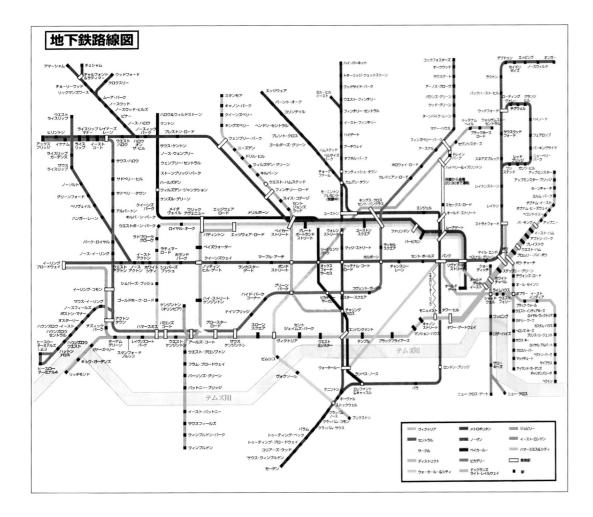

地下鉄路線図

Above: *With no Latin characters in sight, the map in the Japanese 1996 Shobunsha Individual Travel guide looks very strange. Transliteration is a difficult art, and it is unlikely that Transport for London would have been able to offer such a service. Even so, the base map is clearly the compact diary version that London Transport made available during the 1970s and 1980s (see also p. 34). Permission was therefore needed before modifying it.*

Northern Line twists and turns southwards from Camden Town to Euston and Kings Cross (p. 45). Combined, these three elements of the layout are the first points to check when assessing the creativity of a 'new, improved' design, especially an octolinear one. From here, such details as the layout of complex interchanges might be scrutinised.

For the vast majority of the maps in this book, they have almost identical configurations to various official designs and dressing them up with, for example, different station and interchange symbols does little to hide this: the basis of each map can readily be identified. With some unofficial works, parentage is less obvious but still identifiable by an expert on the basis of the layout of the lines.

Armed with these insights, it is possible to take a closer look at some of the more unusual unofficial maps that have appeared in the last three decades and decide what it is about them that is different. Creating categories will help organise our thinking and, from this, those maps can be identified whose appearance is merely superficially different from official designs, despite the visual surprise, versus those that are more indicative of genuine creativity. Unfortunately, under this spotlight some of the most interesting attempts whither so that, fundamentally, they are derivative works to which camouflage has been applied as an attempt at distraction from this.

Ambience. The overall look-and-feel of a map is easy to modify in superficial ways, independently of its design rules and configuration. The basic parameters of the Underground map are so established that any changes, such as using different symbols to denote stations and interchanges or changing the font or the line stroke width, can render it barely recognizable, On the other hand, many tourists unfamiliar with the official design might find a map easier to use if it conformed to the information design traditions of its country of origin. But surface parameters are exactly that and it is the configuration of the lines that forms the basis of the intellectual property. Merely dressing the same configuration up in a different way might change the recognisability of the origin of a map (to a casual glance) but not its legal status.

Colours. Metro systems usually have colour-coded lines and some networks, such as the Chicago L and Washington, DC Metro, name them in this way (hence *Red Line, Orange Line* etc.). With colour an integral component of wayfinding and branding worldwide it seems perverse to create an Underground map in which the line colours are changed so that their appearance is in conflict with the information on the ground. And yet, several designers have done exactly that. Of course, if the colours are changed, then the overall look-and-feel of the design is modified, too, but the key point here is that those aspects that have been categorised as *ambience* (above) can be manipulated independently of the line colours.

Language. For people not used to the Latin alphabet, transliterating Underground station names into familiar characters might give a better idea of how these should be pronounced, although perfect results are often impossible. An Underground map with no recognisable words takes a distinctly unworldly appearance. The intentions of tourist guide publishers who create these maps, derived from official versions, is probably benign – they are providing a useful service for their readers – but this does not alter the fact that intellectual property might have been modified and re-published without permission.

Embellishments. One recurring theme in mapping the railways is the tension between opposite extremes: giving the user the minimum information necessary to plan a journey from A to B versus festooning a map with extra details for orientation, such as streets, parks, tourist attractions and landmarks. Some international airports lie beyond the Underground, and so adding long distance railway links to Gatwick and Stansted might also be useful. Similarly, some attractions cannot be reached by Underground (e.g., Hampton Court), or else only reached circuitously (e.g., Greenwich). Even so, the addition of original details to an already-existing design does not get around intellectual property issues. The base map is copyright, and should not be amended without requesting the consent of the owner of the design.

Proportions. The inside cover of a tourist guide is often the preferred location for an Underground map but the typical proportions of this space (shallow/wide) do not match the natural proportions of the network. In which case, a cut-down version might be offered but, if the preference is to show the full network, then the map might need to be redrawn with angles shallower than 45°. Some guidebooks have covers that unfold to reveal a square page and one way to make full use of this is to redraw the map taller, giving diagonals steeper than 45°. The redrawn map fulfils a space requirement that is not necessarily catered for by official maps but merely stretching or squeezing an already-existing piece of work does not create a new, original design.

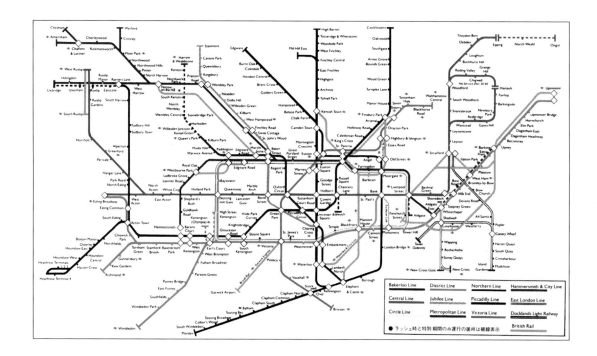

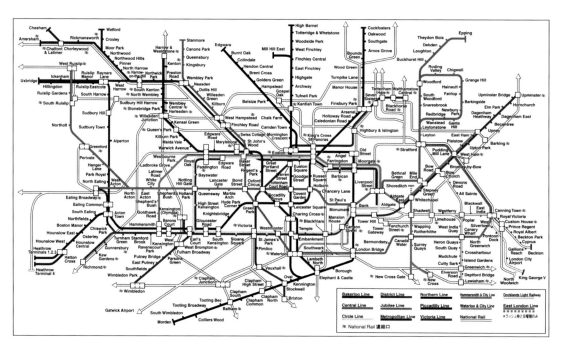

Left and below left: *Maps from the Japanese Red Directory. Despite the compression of south London, these are obvious derivative works but each has additional information. The 1993 map included British Rail lines on which Underground tickets were valid. The 2007 map has more rail lines, and fast routes to Greenwich and Wimbledon can now be identified. A person who makes substantial changes to an existing work might assert that these are sufficiently original to be worthy of copyright. However, this does not nullify the rights of the owner of the base design.*

Right: *In a tourist guide, a natural place for an Underground map is inside the cover. If a folded page is used, this gives a large square space, exactly as available in the Italian 2003 Giunti guide. To fit this, a vertically elongated map was created with diagonals at 59° to horizontal. However, this map also bends in the same ways, at all the same places, as the official version, making it hard to argue that it is an original design. Not only this but the elongation is so excessive that the extremities of the network have been cut off, unlike the maps on pp. 40–41.*

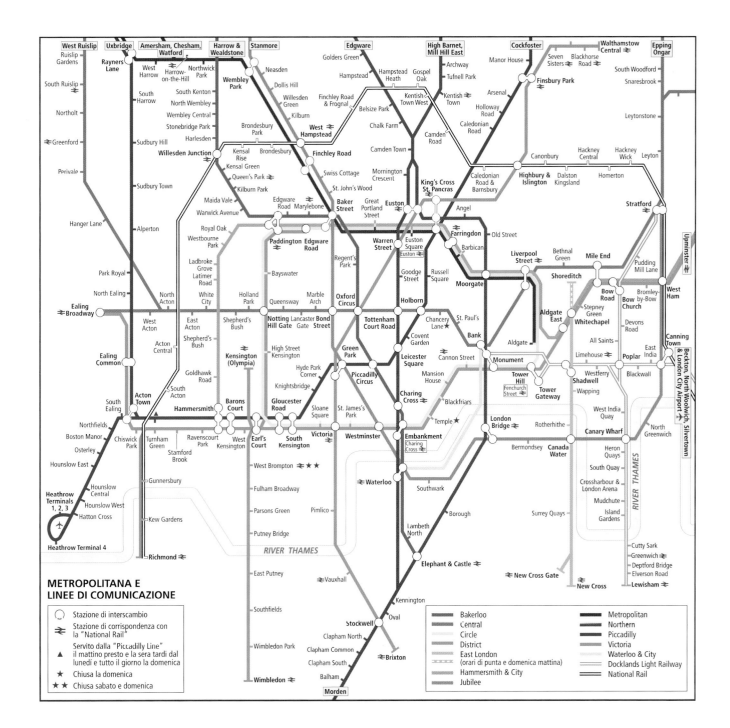

METROPOLITANA E
LINEE DI COMUNICAZIONE

Stazione di interscambio
Stazione di corrispondenza con la "National Rail"
Servito dalla "Piccadilly Line" il mattino presto e la sera tardi dal lunedì e tutto il giorno la domenica
★ Chiusa la domenica
★★ Chiusa sabato e domenica

Bakerloo — Metropolitan
Central — Northern
Circle — Piccadilly
District — Victoria
East London (orari di punta e domenica mattina) — Waterloo & City
Hammersmith & City — Docklands Light Railway
Jubilee — National Rail

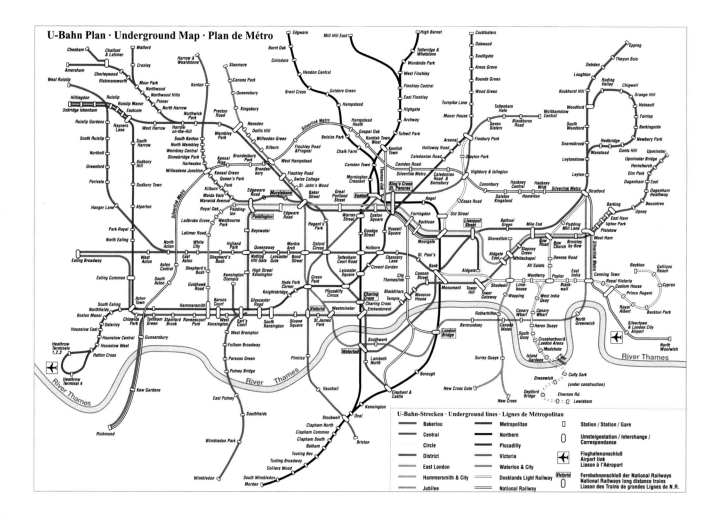

U-Bahn Plan · Underground Map · Plan de Métro

U-Bahn-Strecken · Underground lines · Lignes de Métropolitan

Bakerloo	Metropolitan	Station / Station / Gare
Central	Northern	Umsteigestation / Interchange / Correspondance
Circle	Piccadilly	
District	Victoria	Flughafenanschluß Airport link Liason à l'Aéroport
East London	Waterloo & City	
Hammersmith & City	Docklands Light Railway	Fernbahnanschluß der National Railways National Railways long distance trains Liason des Trains de grandes Lignes de N.R.
Jubilee	National Railway	

Left: *Ever since 1933, the official Underground map has been a strictly linear diagram. In other words, only straight lines are permitted, linked by tightly radiused curves. The design included in the German 2001 Marco Polo folding street map of London breaks the rules spectacularly. Curves dominate and yet, because of the topographical distortion, this still counts as a diagram. This design was massively influential on the author's own work (p. 92). However, take a close look at it. The bottle-shape Circle Line is obvious, and also the Central Line dive-down at Bank. The Northern Line curves at Euston mirror the official version on p. 63 even if they do not follow them faithfully. The inescapable inference is that, despite the unusual design rules, these are merely camouflaging the origins of this map rather than providing a means for the designer to attempt a creative new method in order to improve usability.*

Design Rules. The official Underground diagram has always been octolinear. Furthermore, only rarely has the diagonal angle not been 45° (60° from 1940 to 1941, 42° from 1961 to 1963). Some unofficial maps depart from this, perhaps using multiple diagonal angles or curvilinear lines only. Once traditional methods are put to one side – for example, in an attempt to be better able to achieve design priorities – explorations of the potential of rule-breaking maps can yield fascinating insights into visual information design (see Chapter 6). However, using alternative design rules can create maps with very alien appearance and, therefore, this can be a useful method for concealing the underlying origins of a derivative work. That

such attempts are rarely successful is a testament to the distinctiveness of the official Underground map.

Design. Irrespective of whether or not unusual design rules are adopted, the best way not to violate copyright is to start with a clean slate, attempting something genuinely original. Although there might be some similarities to official versions there should be enough divergence for originality to be plausible. However, evaluating whether there is *sufficient* originality is particularly difficult because of the problem of configural convergence. For a designer, it is safest only to refer to topographical maps, avoiding any temptation to view official versions. Hence, if there is an accusation of plagiarism, it should be possible to argue

Right: *The map from the Japanese 2007 Seibido Shuppan guide: A Wonderful Travel – Joy of City Walking has not only non-standard design rules but an attempt has also been made to create an original work, with a topographical centre and schematised suburbs, similar in concept to the design on p. 28. Even so, some suburban configurations are very reminiscent of the official map, despite their horizontal compression and vertical elongation. [27 by 21 cm]*

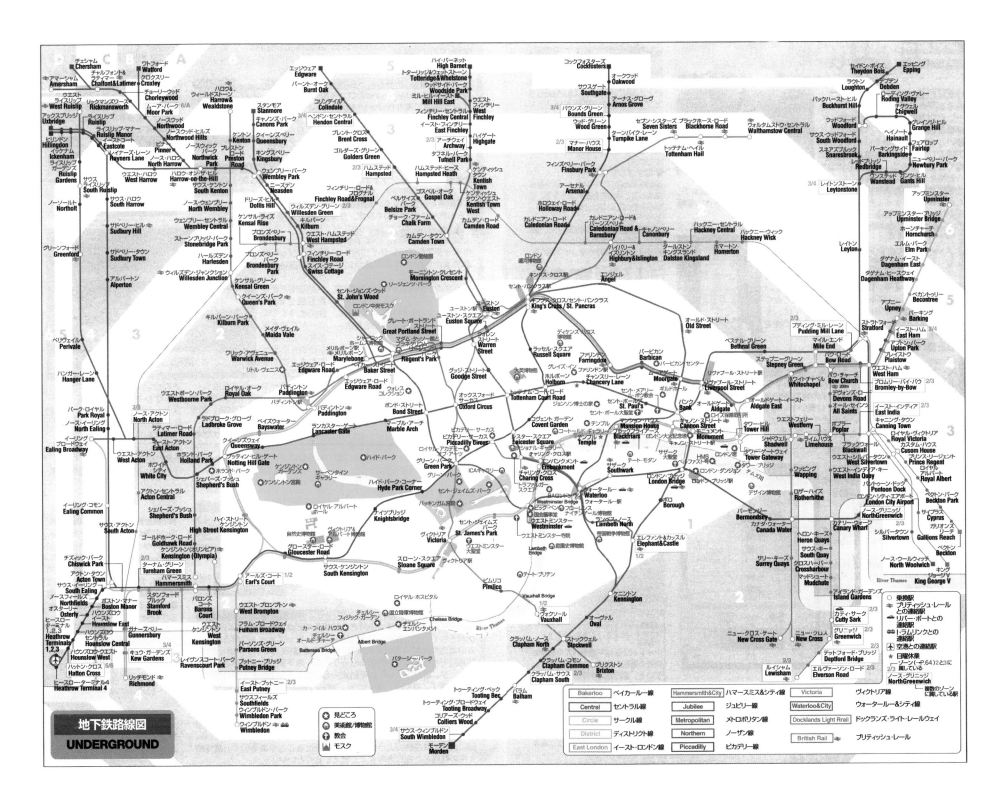

地下鉄路線図
UNDERGROUND

Left: *The design included in the Austrian 2011 Freytag & Berndt folding street map of London is hard to describe except by resorting to colloquialisms. One has to wonder whether anyone has ever used it successfully to plan a journey. Even so, the bottle-shaped Circle Line, Central Line dive down at Bank, and twists at Euston are plain to see. The layout at Earl's Court is another giveaway, depicted on official designs from 2002 to 2009. If a map is sufficiently derivative, no amount of madness can hide the motivation of the designer.*

that the mechanics of the design process inevitably leads to particular configurations in some circumstances.

Disorder. Occasionally, maps will surface which have the expected symbols and line colours; landscape proportions; no unusual embellishments; and the standard octolinear

angles and yet they still look distinctive, often for the wrong reasons. Maps that are in this category (the one on p. 60 also qualifies) are somewhat misproportioned in terms of the size of lettering and the space available to apply it, with the designers resorting to rotated text in an

Right: *Often multiple methods of camouflage are used. The design in the USA 1998 Rand & McNally folding street map of London has changed ambience, line colours and design rules (not all diagonals are 45°). The gapped stations are distinctive but the configuration is still recognisable. [30 by 21 cm]*

Below: *The map from the Russian 2013 Pareto-Print Red Guide also has seemingly randomised colours and, simultaneously, has changed ambience with distinctive pointed station markers but, again, to no avail. The layout at Earl's Court indicates that the official base map was similar to the one used for the design on the facing page. Indeed, the layout at West Hampstead pinpoints this to one of the official maps from 2008.*

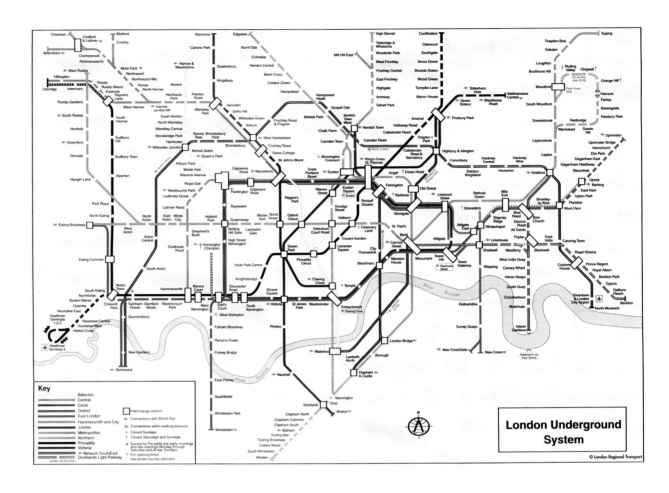

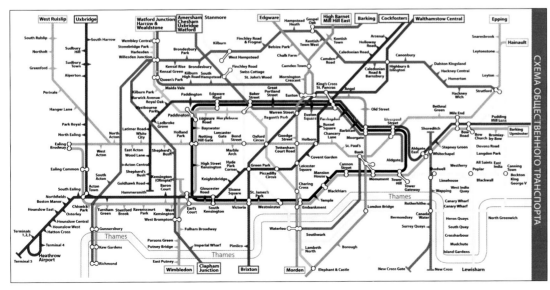

attempt to place station names. The resulting chaos can only result in severe usability issues but, even faced with this, it can still be possible to identify the originals from which the works were derived.

Looking at most of the maps in the current chapter, it is a sad but inescapable conclusion that many of the designers knew that they were essentially copying official versions and merely had subterfuge as their design priority. In the process, they applied a number of superficial tricks that concealed their wrongdoing, although it should be noted that, in some instances, derivative works might have been the product of benign intentions. Even so, much of the creativity manifested has been in the application of camouflage techniques rather than the production of original work. However, there are some exceptions to this,

71

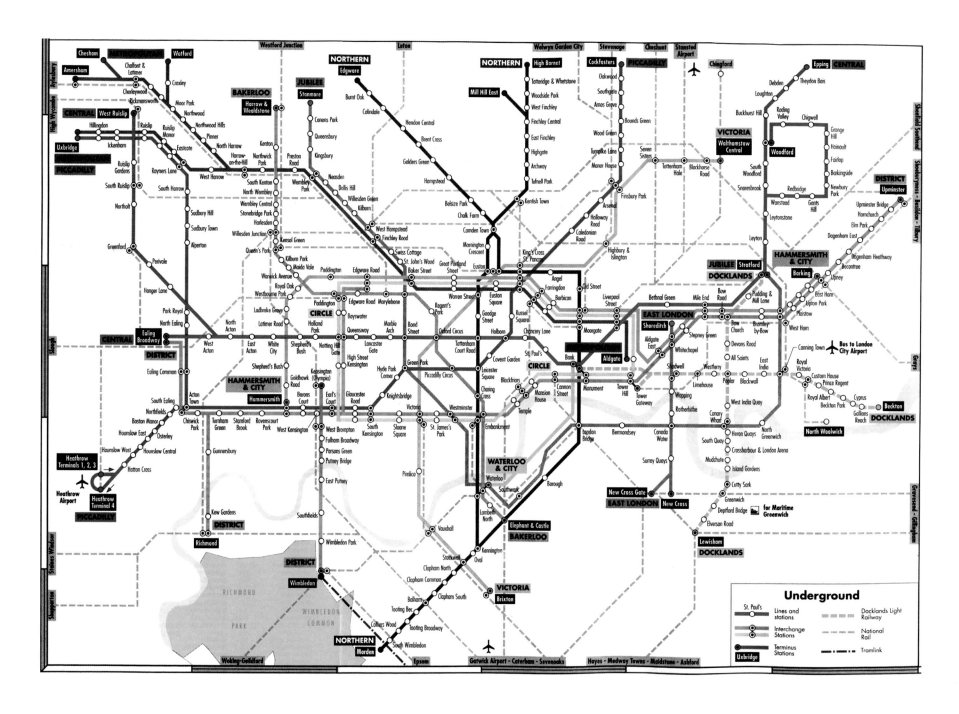

with results that give pause for thought. Furthermore, with today's availability of computers with power that could only be dreamt of a couple of decades ago, there is a small army of designers who are interested in exploring the possibilities of genuinely novel approaches to map design, pushing the envelope to see what can be achieved. Generally, these do not appear in guidebooks but, thanks to the Internet, they can still enjoy a wide audience.

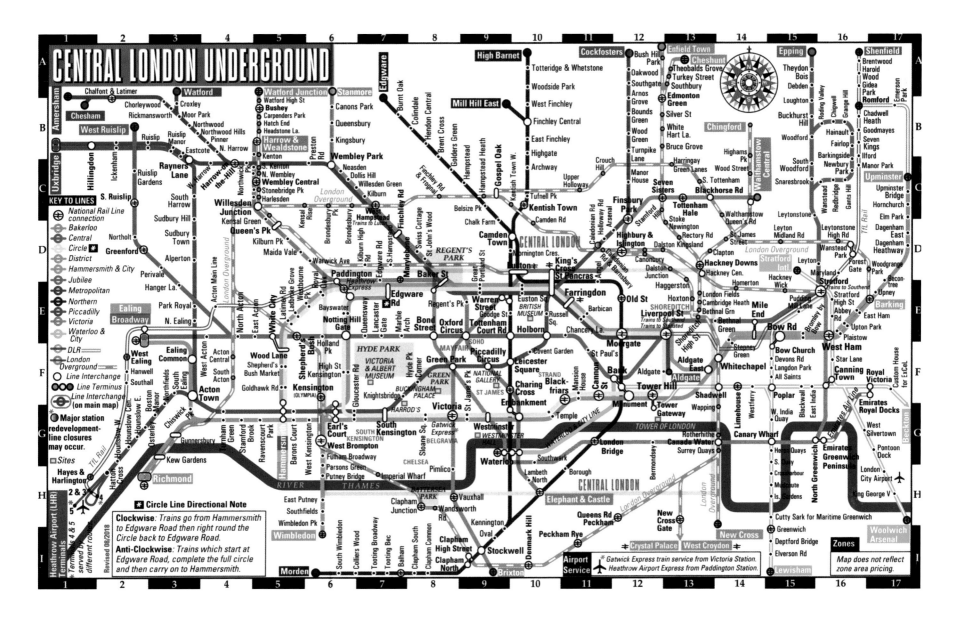

CENTRAL LONDON UNDERGROUND

Left: *The design included in the French 2006 IGN folding map of London features both altered ambience and embellishments, as well as a few rogue angles, giving it an unusual appearance. However, the inclusion of just one park area seems strange and the layout at many junctions, in particular Earl's Court and Poplar, are confusing. The value of including National Rail lines without indicating services, or even stations, is questionable. The configural hallmarks of a derivative work are all present.*

Above: *The USA 2018 Streetwise Underground map, available as a standalone purchase, is harder to judge for originality. It differs in ambience, embellishments and design rules. Some aspects of its layout are similar to official maps, such as the Central Line dive down, but not others, such as at Euston. It might be an example of divergence, where original resemblance to an official design has become diluted with modifications over time.* © Michelin et Cie, 2018, ISBN 9782067230019

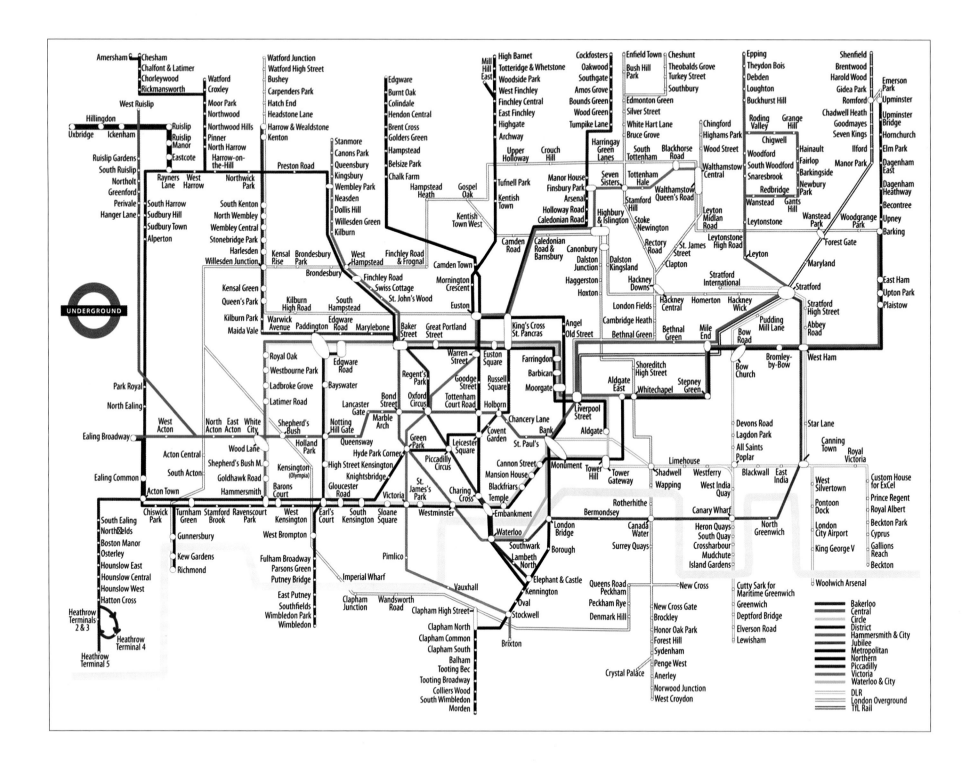

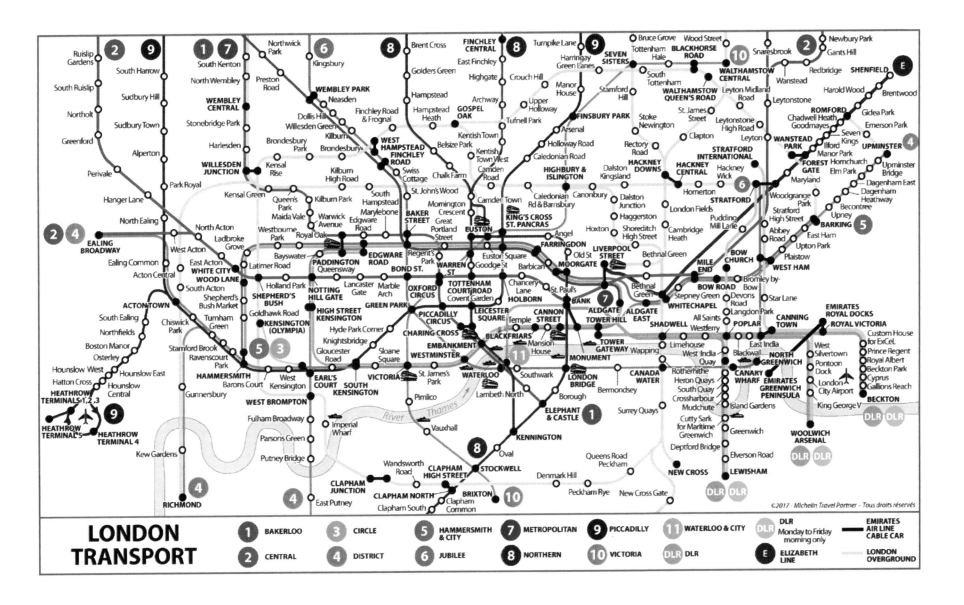

LONDON TRANSPORT

1 BAKERLOO	3 CIRCLE	5 HAMMERSMITH & CITY	7 METROPOLITAN	9 PICCADILLY	11 WATERLOO & CITY	DLR DLR Monday to Friday morning only	EMIRATES AIR LINE CABLE CAR
2 CENTRAL	4 DISTRICT	6 JUBILEE	8 NORTHERN	10 VICTORIA	DLR DLR	E ELIZABETH LINE	LONDON OVERGROUND

©2017 - Michelin Travel Partner – Tous droits réservés

Left: *The map from the Austrian 2016 Lonitzberg guide is a challenge to design sensibilities. It is part dominated by a grid of horizontal and vertical lines but is punctuated by diagonals at seemingly random angles. Configurations that are identical to the official map, especially at the centre, jostle for position with ones that differ. Whether this design displays sufficient originality not to be classed as a derivative work is open to debate, inappropriate use of the roundel is not. [29 by 21 cm]*

Above: *The map in the Dutch 2018 Michelin Groene Reisegids Londen Weekend possibly has the most original layout of the diagrams in this chapter. The Central Line dive down is present but the Circle Line departs subtly from a bottle-shape, and there are numerous other differences in configuration. However, the yellow London Overground lines are difficult to distinguish and the line to Shenfield is incorrectly shown as stopping at Whitechapel. © Michelin et Cie, 2018, ISBN 9789401439725*

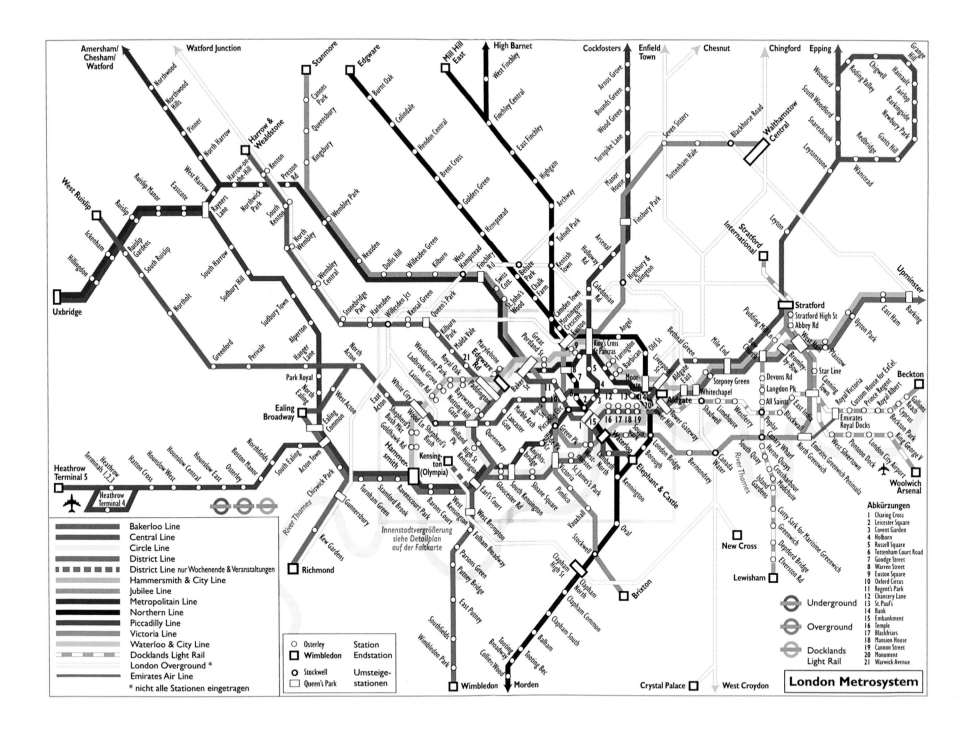

London Metrosystem

Bakerloo Line
Central Line
Circle Line
District Line
District Line nur Wochenende & Veranstaltungen
Hammersmith & City Line
Jubilee Line
Metropolitain Line
Northern Line
Piccadilly Line
Victoria Line
Waterloo & City Line
Docklands Light Rail
London Overground *
Emirates Air Line
* nicht alle Stationen eingetragen

○ Osterley — Station
◻ Wimbledon — Endstation
◉ Stockwell — Umsteige-
◻ Queen's Park — stationen

Innenstadtvergrößerung
siehe Detailplan
auf der Faltkarte

Abkürzungen
1 Charing Cross
2 Leicester Square
3 Covent Garden
4 Holborn
5 Russell Square
6 Tottenham Court Road
7 Goodge Street
8 Warren Street
9 Euston Square
10 Oxford Circus
11 Regent's Park
12 Chancery Lane
13 St. Paul's
14 Bank
15 Embankment
16 Temple
17 Blackfriars
18 Mansion House
19 Cannon Street
20 Monument
21 Warwick Avenue

⊖ Underground
⊖ Overground
⊖ Docklands
Light Rail

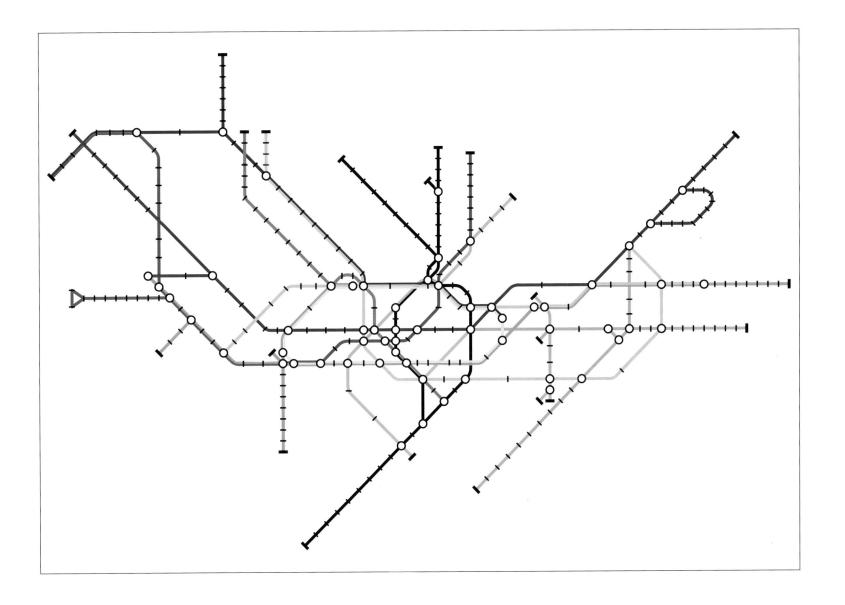

Left: *The map from the German 2016 Iwanowski guide is intended to be topographically representative, hence the small central area that requires a numbered key. It is definitely not based on official Underground maps, despite the inappropriate use of roundels. However, it is questionable whether the attempt at topographical accuracy, in the absence of surface features against which to orientate, is beneficial to the user. Also, the diagonals are not quite at consistent angles, adding to the disorder created by the rotated text.*

Above: *An octolinear map that cannot be said to be derivative of official versions. The reason is that this 2019 diagram, courtesy of Martin Nöllenburg and Soeren Nickel at TU Wien, is computer-generated with no human input. The software is given the GPS co-ordinates of the stations, the lines served and general guidelines on criteria for effective design, and it creates a layout that attempts to maximise satisfaction of the criteria. The algorithms were developed by Martin Nöllenburg and Alexander Wolff at Universität Würzburg. Only the Underground and Docklands Light Railway are mapped here, comparable to the official map on p. 63. Computers currently struggle with large networks and with naming stations, but are steadily improving.*

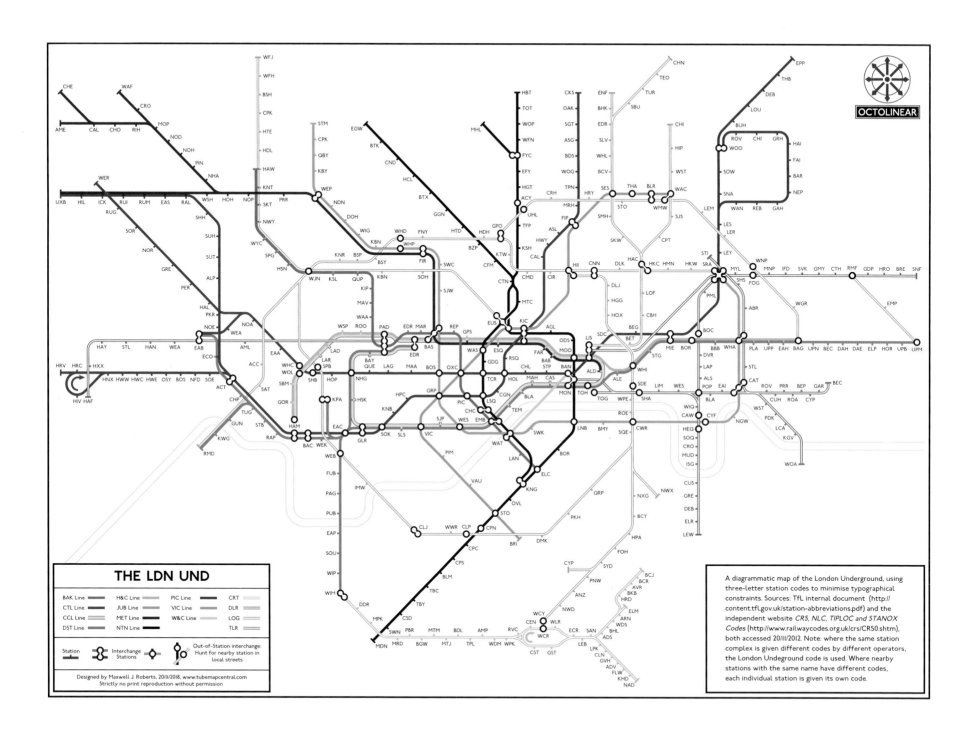

THE LDN UND

Designed by Maxwell J. Roberts, 20/11/2018, www.tubemapcentral.com
Strictly no print reproduction without permission

BAK Line	H&C Line	PIC Line	CRT	
CTL Line	JUB Line	VIC Line	DLR	
CCL Line	MET Line	W&C Line	LOG	
DST Line	NTN Line		TLR	

Station | Interchange Stations | | Out-of-Station interchange: Hunt for nearby station in local streets

A diagrammatic map of the London Underground, using three-letter station codes to minimise typographical constraints. Sources: TfL internal document (http://content.tfl.gov.uk/station-abbreviations.pdf) and the independent website *CRS, NLC, TIPLOC and STANOX Codes* (http://www.railwaycodes.org.uk/crs/CRS0.shtm), both accessed 20/11/2012. Note: where the same station complex is given different codes by different operators, the London Undelgnod code is used. Where nearby stations with the same name have different codes, each individual station is given its own code.

OctoLINEAR

Chapter Six

Pushing the Envelope

WHY IS THE OFFICIAL UNDERGROUND MAP designed the way it is today? Just because certain design rules were successfully applied in 1933, does that mean that these are the best ones to use for London? For every other network in the world? What other ways might there be for designing a map? With ever-increasing network complexity, might any of the alternatives result in a more effective design? Questions such as these have attracted the attention of many people and, with today's computers, they are in a better position to investigate them than ever before and make their attempts available to the world at the click of a mouse.

As soon as anyone tries to create a schematic map, whatever the city, the challenges of the task soon become obvious. To maximise usability, a map should have simple line trajectories which should relate together coherently to give the overall design good shape. It should also be balanced – avoiding empty space in the vicinity of crushed-together stations – and aesthetically pleasing. Distorting topography is permissible but care is needed so that the layouts on the map do not mislead people into planning poor journeys, for example going the 'long way round' or travelling by Underground when it might have been quicker to walk.

In attempting to create the perfect layout the designer will encounter other issues, such as how best to format lines and stations and to what extent should service patterns be shown. Interchange symbols need to be clear and not lead to unintended inferences about, for example, how long a walk might be required to change trains: human beings have remarkable ability to go beyond information given. The novice designer will soon learn just how much difficulty is presented by long station names and the ways in which they constrain solutions at difficult parts of the map. Any supplementary information should be consistently applied, logical and correct, so that users are informed without being distracted.

Some of the basic design criteria are in opposition to each other: simple line trajectories are often created at the cost of topographical distortion and people vary in their tolerance for this. Some complain even when this could not conceivably matter, for example, wanting accurate twists and turns of a line in a remote suburb, even though there are no other ones nearby to offer alternative routes. Any aesthetic criterion is likewise going to be subject to individual differences. It seems almost impossible to design a map that everyone hates (the author has tried, and failed). And, of course, beauty is in the eye of the designer, perhaps sometimes leading to maps being released to the world when the parent should have been more cautious, although the ghoulish charm of a truly awful design, naively put forward by an inexperienced designer as the answer to imaginary problems, is undeniable. None of the maps reproduced in this chapter comes into this category.

With all the difficulties presented by creating a complex schematic map, why do people try? There is, of course, the rising to the challenge, the curiosity about how a familiar artefact might appear in a different design universe, and the satisfaction of creating something truly original. Behind all these rewards comes similar motivation: for people prepared to look closely it is easy to criticise the design of recent official Underground maps. In 1933, east London was mapped only as far as Bow (p. 14). Eighty-five years later, over two hundred extra stations are shown and yet the dimensions of the pocket version have remained almost the same. The result of squeezing in everything is twisted line trajectories, stations crowded together, a tiny font and bizarre topographical space-warps. Objectively, the official map fails the criteria for effective design.

Perhaps the most straightforward challenge is to see what can be achieved within the realms of the standard design rules: octolinear angles – horizontal and vertical lines and 45° diagonals. Beyond expanding the size of the map to give the network an opportunity to breathe,

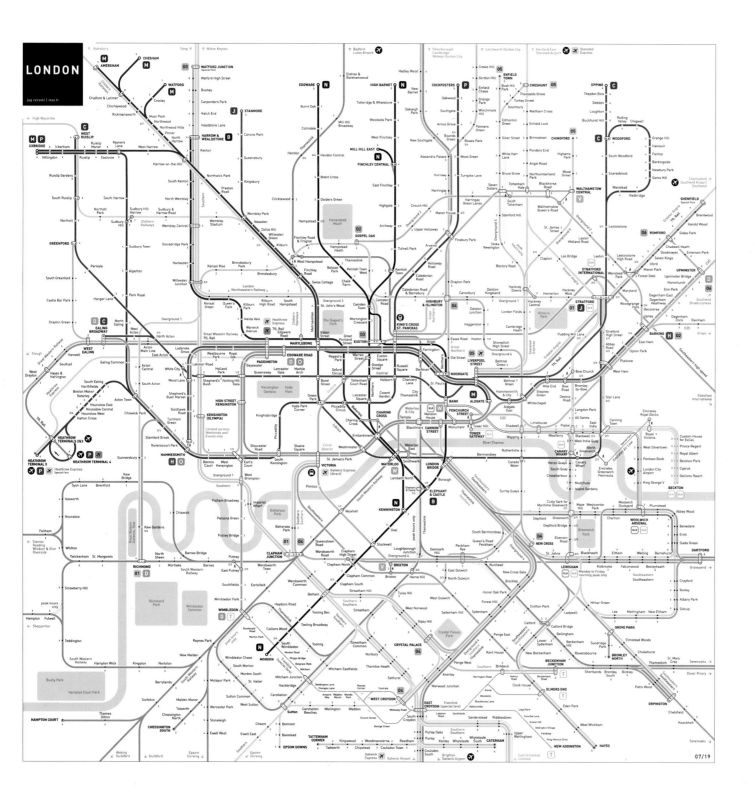

Left: Designer Jug Cerovic seeks to unify the look-and-feel of all urban rail maps worldwide, using octolinear angles along with standardised stroke widths, typography, colour palette and symbols (a standard he has named INAT). In practice, for London, this means gentler curve radii than on the official map and the loss of the famous Johnston lettering. Beyond the Underground network, the inclusion of the other railways of London challenges the overall clarity of any map. This 2019 design shows them in muted tones, mitigating the effect of the added complexity, and is reminiscent of the very first official Underground map (p. 9). It is noteworthy how much of north London is dominated by verticals and south London by diagonal lines.

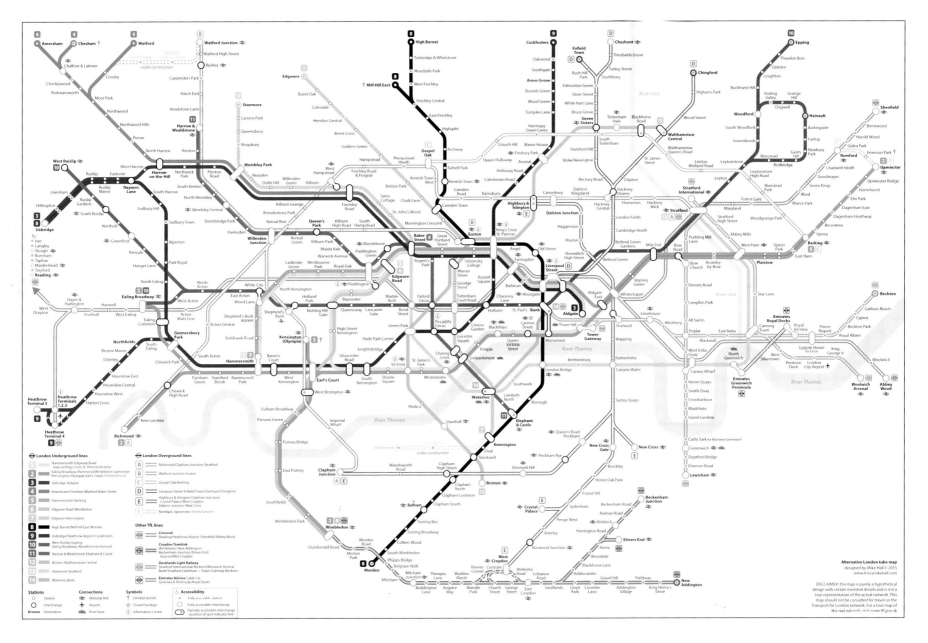

Above: *This 2015 octolinear design by Mike Hall is most immediately striking for its more topographically accurate Circle Line, dispensing with the classic thermos flask shape. It also experiments with depicting service patterns on the Metropolitan and District Lines, and colour-coding the London Overground services to show their organisation. The thicker lines and station dots give it a very North American look, reminiscent of Boston T, Chicago L and New York City Subway networks*

experiments with typography, such as rotated text, allowing lettering to interrupt lines and shortened station names, all allow the design priorities to be attained with fewer compromises necessary. However, there is no intrinsic reason why the traditional look-and-feel of the official Underground map needs to be maintained. Stroke widths for lines can be varied, curve radii can be relaxed and the station symbols need not be tickmarks. With the Crossrail *Elizabeth Line* set to introduce to Londoners yet more vast underground citadels of joined stations, linked-circle

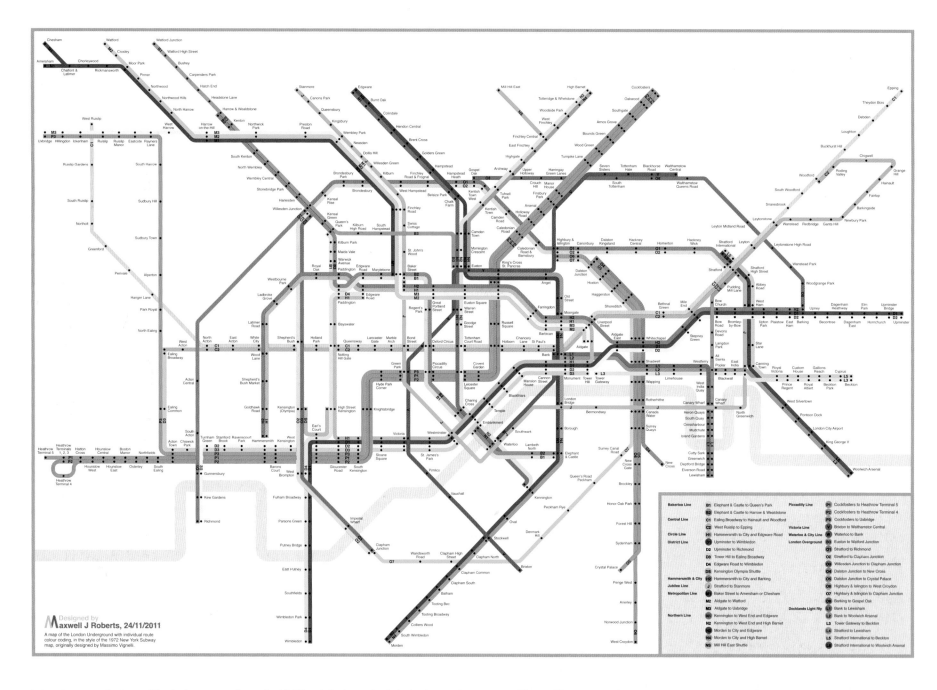

A map of the London Underground with individual route colour coding, in the style of the 1972 New York Subway map, originally designed by Massimo Vignelli.

interchanges, first used in their current form in 1963, might have had their day and more sophisticated, informative notation could be needed.

Another avenue to explore is the tension between topographical accuracy versus simplicity of line trajectories. Few people realise just how disorganised London's network really is and just how unsuited it is to octolinear angles, hence the need

Above: *This 2011 octolinear map by the author shows the London network in the style of Massimo Vignelli's 1972 New York City Subway diagram. Quite apart from the fascination of seeing London in such an other-worldly way, this demonstrates how a methodology that might function for one city may not be well-suited to another.*

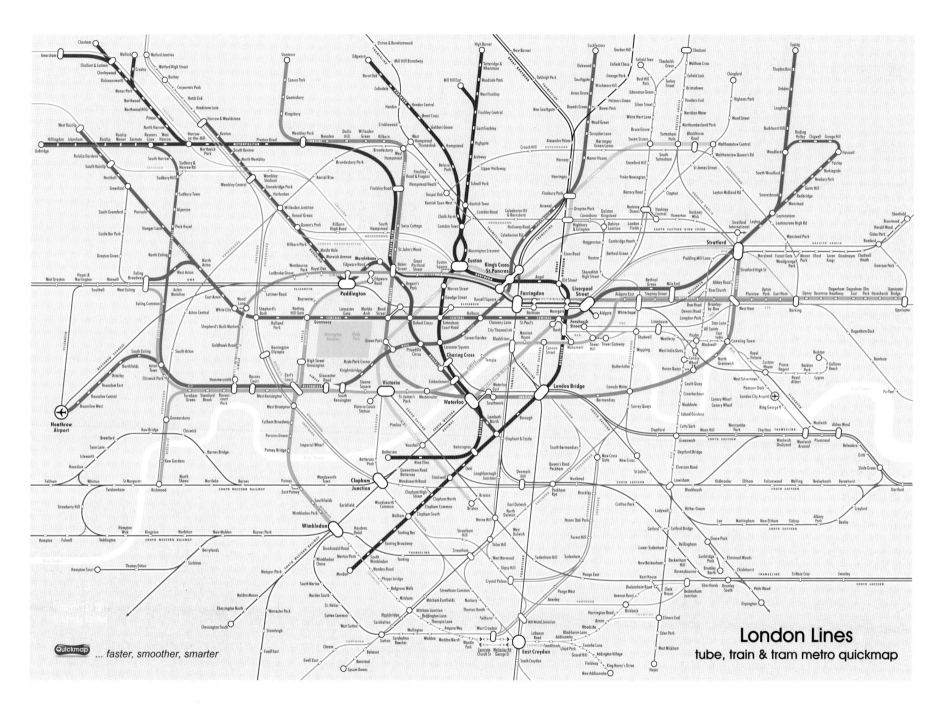

London Lines
tube, train & tram metro quickmap

Above: *Few maps are able to match the aplomb of Quickmap (2019) in using gentle curves to link straight segments. The slightly off-vertical lines are intended to emphasise the feeling of dynamic flow. The complexity of the non-Underground lines is tamed using a thinner stroke.* for compromise between various opposing forces on the official map. On the other hand, what might be possible if a more relaxed attitude is taken to topographical accuracy? Might the payback in simplicity of line trajectories warrant this? At what point do the costs of topographical distortion outweigh the benefits?

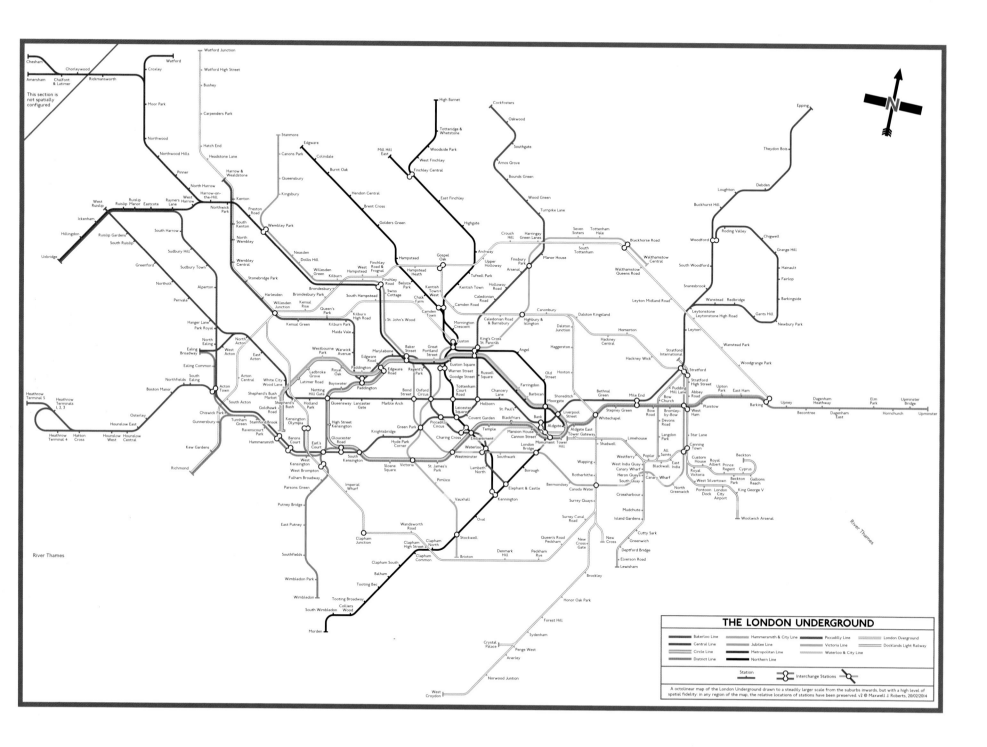

THE LONDON UNDERGROUND

Bakerloo Line	Hammersmith & City Line	Piccadilly Line	London Overground
Central Line	Jubilee Line	Victoria Line	Docklands Light Railway
Circle Line	Metropolitan Line	Waterloo & City Line	
District Line	Northern Line		

Station   Interchange Stations

A octolinear map of the London Underground drawn to a steadily larger scale from the suburbs inwards, but with a high level of spatial fidelity: in any region of the map, the relative locations of stations have been preserved. v2 © Maxwell J. Roberts, 20/02/2014

Left: *This 2014 octolinear design by the author enlarges central London, but maintains accurate relative spatial positions of stations throughout. To achieve this without errors or bias, a mathematical transformation was applied to a geographical map and then the meandering lines were straightened. The chaos would have been even worse if the geographical map had not been rotated 12.5° clockwise first, hence the north point. The variable scale might be misleading in places. For example, walking from Watford to Watford Junction is much farther than Paddington to Marble Arch. The disorder of London is a barrier to a simple, coherent, attractive design, hence the more conventional maps have simplified line trajectories alongside topographical distortion.*

Right: *The first London map by Jug Cerovic, in his standardised octolinear style, was published in 2014. Here, not only is there considerable topographical distortion but there is even some topological distortion, too, such as in west London where the Central Line fails to cross the Metropolitan Line. The designer calls this the Mark IV map, not because it was his fourth attempt but because the shape of the Circle Line is reminiscent of the British First World War tank.*

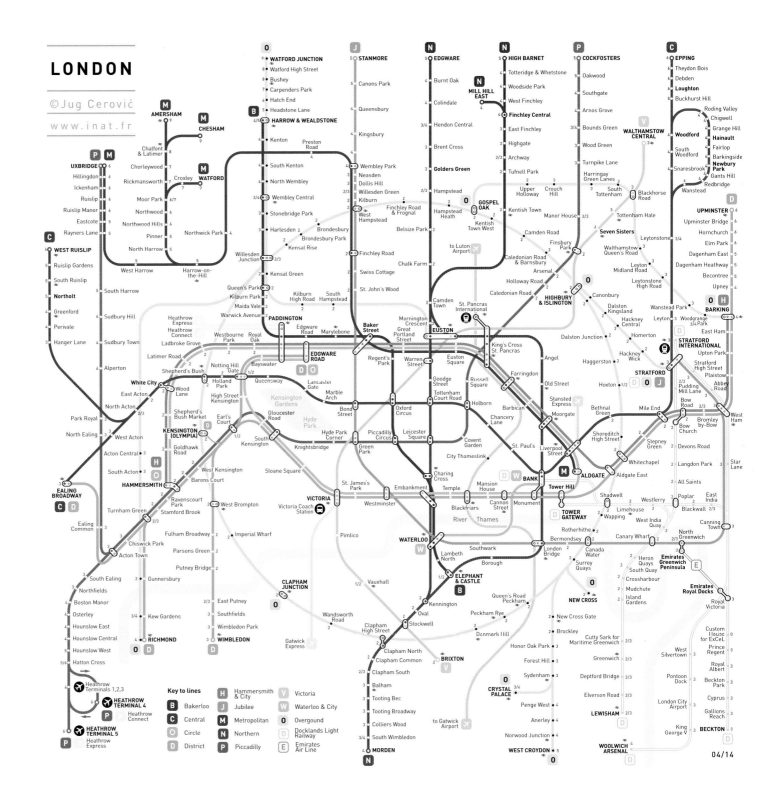

LONDON

© Jug Cerović
www.inat.fr

Key to lines

H	Hammersmith & City	**V**	Victoria
B	Bakerloo	**W**	Waterloo & City
C	Central	**O**	Overground
O	Circle	**D**	Docklands Light Railway
M	Metropolitan	**E**	Emirates Air Line
N	Northern		
P	Piccadilly		

04/14

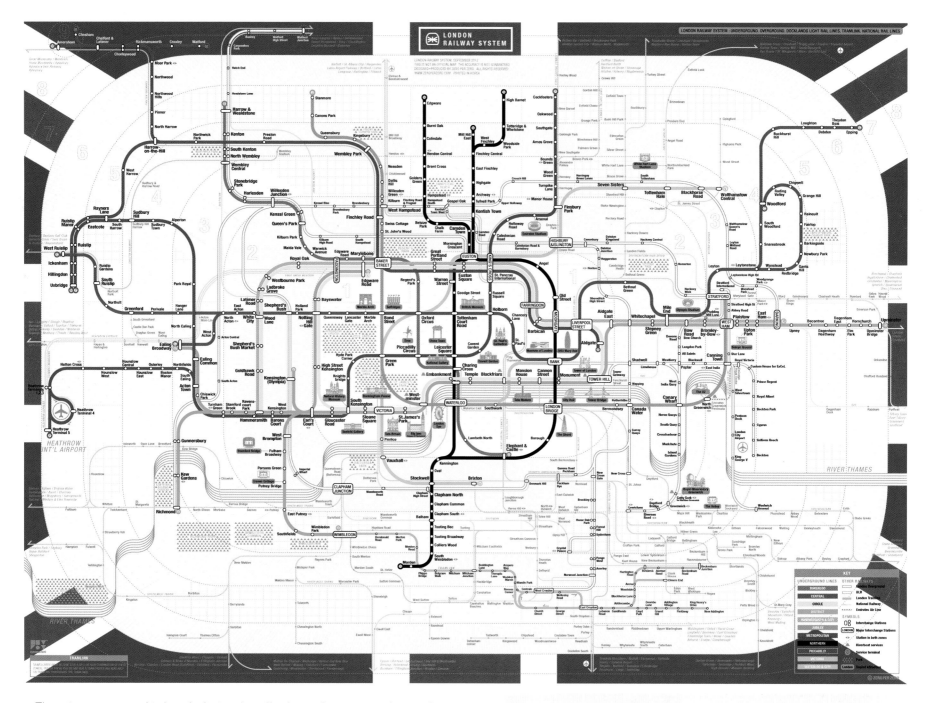

There is no cartographic law declaring that all urban rail maps must be octolinear, and no psychological findings to imply this either. In theory, any set of angles could be applied. Using fewer angles can be surprisingly effective: the reduced flexibility need not necessarily penalise the designer. Exceeding octolinearity, with five or

Above: *This 2012 map by Zero per Zero studios has only two angles: horizontal and vertical lines, making it tetralinear. Such maps can appear harsh but this is prevented here by effective use of gently radiused corners. Plenty of tourist attractions have been added. [52 by 38 cm]*

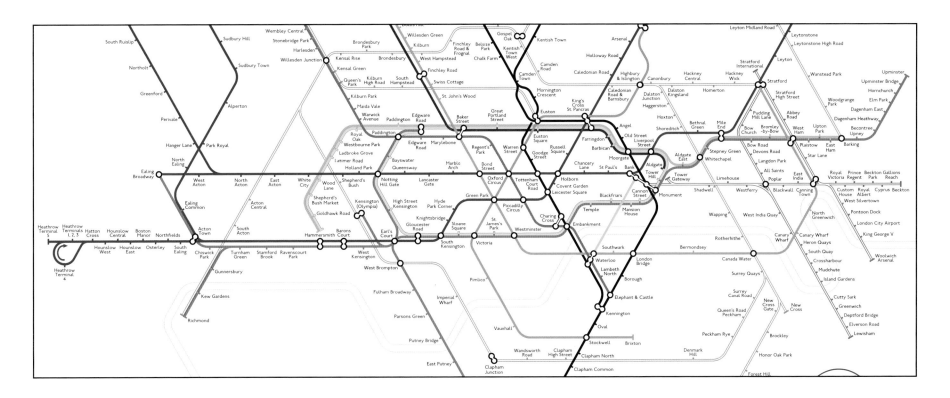

Above: *Is London a hexalinear city? This 2011 design by the author seems to suggest that three angles could be sufficient. It has simple straight lines inside the Circle Line – fewer bends than can be achieved with octolinear angles – and equilateral triangles to please fans of geometry.*

Right: *However, it is important to choose the correct hexalinear angles: one rotation prohibits horizontal lines and one prohibits verticals. Without horizontal lines available the map of London is a disaster, showing the importance of matching design rules to a city. These two maps are named the* good twin *and the* evil twin.

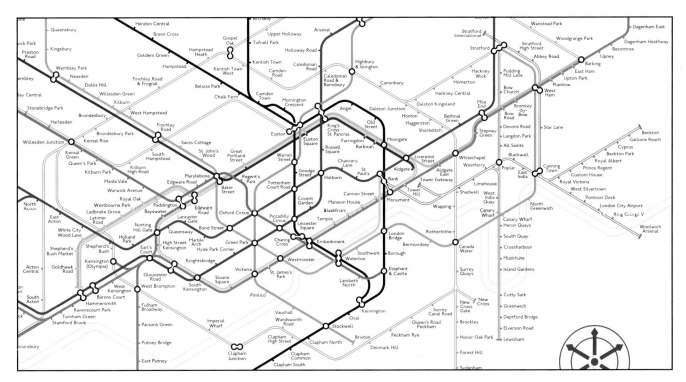

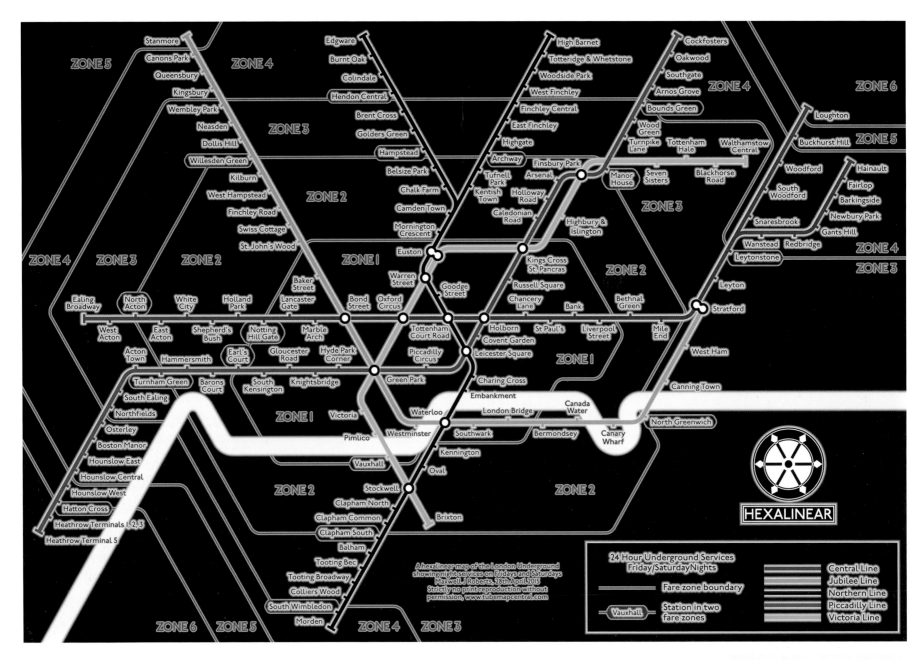

A hexalinear map of the London Underground
showing night services on Fridays and Saturdays
Maxwell J Roberts, 28th April 2015
Strictly no print reproduction without
permission. www.tubemapcentral.com

24 Hour Underground Services
Friday/Saturday Nights

—— Fare zone boundary

Vauxhall   Station in two
            fare zones

| | | | Central Line
| | | | Jubilee Line
| | | | Northern Line
| | | | Piccadilly Line
| | | | Victoria Line

HEXALINEAR

more angles, however, is not for the fainthearted. For these, overall coherence can break down, resulting in a shapeless mess. Large numbers of angles reduce the potential for lines to be parallel and to cross each other perpendicularly. The key to the best maps is that individual line trajectories are not only simple but also that lines relate to each other to bind the design together. Also, if the map does not have strong horizontals on which to ground it visually, users might find it unsettling.

What might be the potential benefits of increasing the available angles (i.e., higher order linearity)? Every designer has experienced the annoyance when an extended line

Above: *Hexalinear angles can have a dynamic effect, highlighted by the black background and backlighting on this 2015 map, by the author, of London's night Underground. Its impact probably exceeds its usability.*

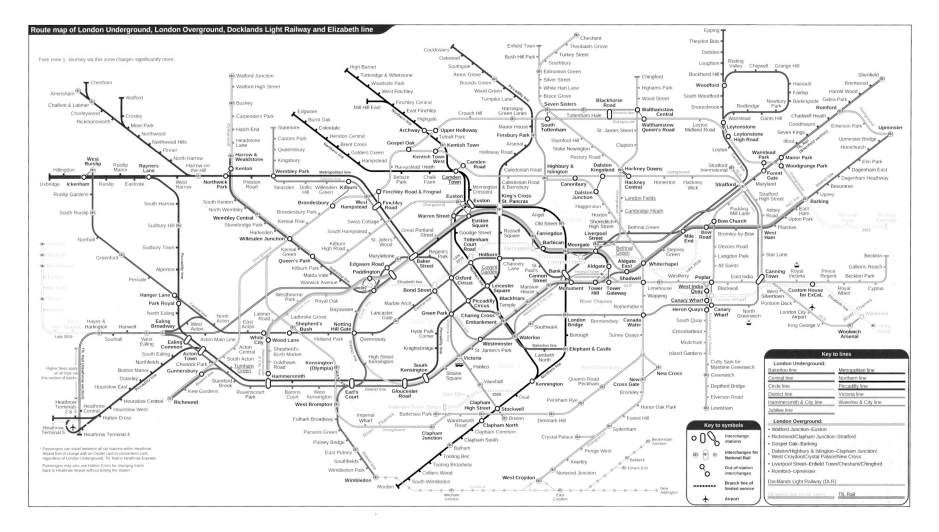

Route map of London Underground, London Overground, Docklands Light Railway and Elizabeth line

Above: *Higher order linearity from 'Sameboat' in 2019. This map uses seven angles; horizontal, vertical, and diagonals derived from the 3-4-5 Pythagorean triangle. In terms of the nomenclature used here, this is a dodecalinear map with irregular angle spacing. The result is very compact, in part owing to the unusual idea of rotating central London to approximately 36°. In reality this is tilted at around 12° and most designers snap it to horizontal.*

does not meet another at the right place. Small deviations can have big consequences, and it might be tempting to bend the rules and rotate the occasional line just a little bit so that the problem is solved. A reckless designer might get away with these ad hoc fixes once or twice, but the map gets messier and harder to rework as a result. Too many angles rotated too much can appear amateurish. Better reasons for higher-order linearity are as follows:

1. **Improved compactness.** With diagonals other than 45° available, it is possible to make the map much shallower or narrower, although station names are hard to place for diagonals much less than 30°.

2. **Improved topographical accuracy.** London is complex and disorganised and, with additional angles, it might be possible better to match straight lines to real-life railways, avoiding the octolinear chaos on p. 84.

3. **Improved simplicity of line trajectories.** Careful use of multiple angles can result in straighter lines than octolinear maps, yet maintaining coherence and also keeping topographical distortion under control.

Irrespective of priorities, such maps are difficult to design because the added freedom increases the possibilities to explore. Also, their less organised appearance and unusual spatial dialect makes many users suspicious of them.

London

PROJECT MAPPING www.projectmapping.co.uk
© 2019 Andrew Smithers London 27 26/9/2019

||||||| Under construction
∞ Interchange
C⊃O Out of station interchange

Overground
Underground

90

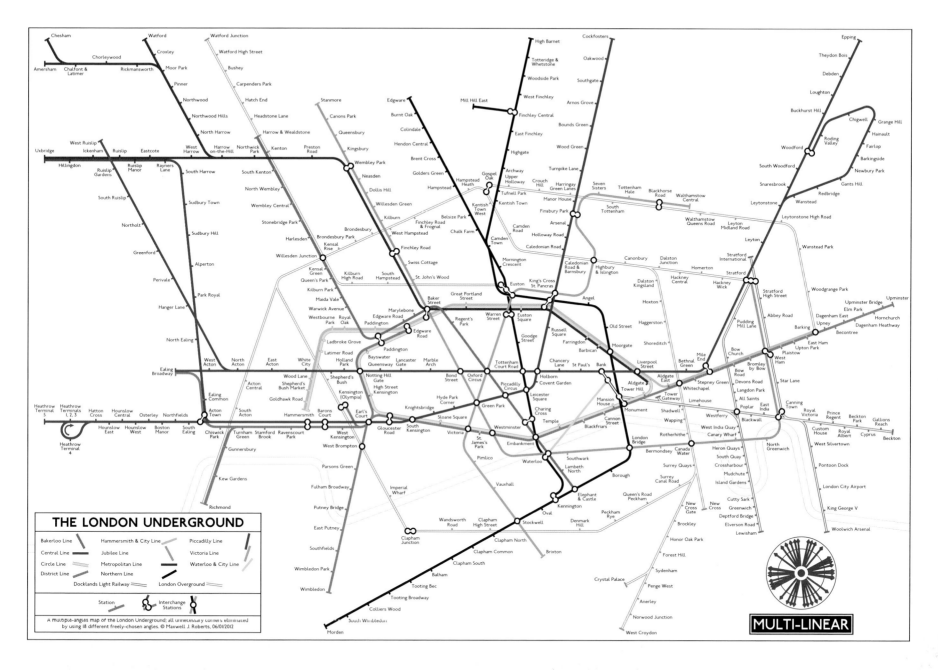

THE LONDON UNDERGROUND

Bakerloo Line	Hammersmith & City Line	Piccadilly Line
Central Line	Jubilee Line	Victoria Line
Circle Line	Metropolitan Line	Waterloo & City Line
District Line	Northern Line	
	Docklands Light Railway	London Overground

Station   Interchange Stations

A multiple-angles map of the London Underground; all unnecessary corners eliminated by using 18 different freely-chosen angles. © Maxwell J. Roberts, 06/01/2012

MULTI-LINEAR

Left: *2019 Underground map by Andrew Smithers of Project Mapping. The author of this book counted at least eleven different angles, making it hard to categorise mathematically except as a multi-linear map. The intention of the designer was that higher order linearity would permit both simpler line trajectories and also good topographical accuracy.*

Above: *A true multi-linear map created by the author in 2012. Any angle is permitted, but it is best to keep these under control. Nineteen angles were needed to achieve the straightest possible line trajectories. Such maps are generally rated by users as being unattractive and, even with the straight Central Line giving a clear axis, this one was no exception.*

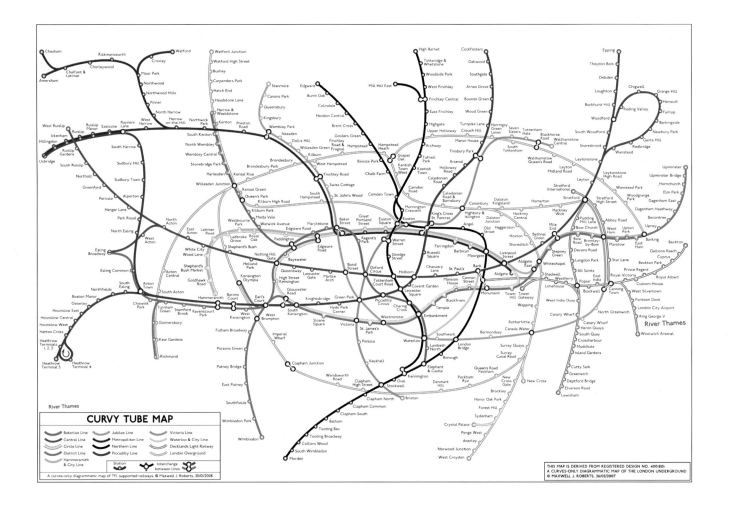

CURVY TUBE MAP

Bakerloo Line • Jubilee Line • Victoria Line
Central Line • Metropolitan Line • Waterloo & City Line
Circle Line • Northern Line • Docklands Light Railway
District Line • Piccadilly Line • London Overground
Hammersmith & City Line • Station • Interchange between lines

A curves-only diagrammatic map of TfL supported railways. © Maxwell J. Roberts, 30/01/2008

THIS MAP IS DERIVED FROM REGISTERED DESIGN NO. 4001801:
A CURVES-ONLY DIAGRAMMATIC MAP OF THE LONDON UNDERGROUND
© MAXWELL J. ROBERTS, 26/02/2007

Left: *London responds well to being converted to straight lines. Even so, a curvilinear approach has achieved some popularity. This 2008 version is the second attempt by the author (see also p. 5). The intention for such designs should be to attempt to make changes in curvature imperceptible so that interruptions to flow are minimised.*

Right: *The first concentric circles map of London was created in 2012 by Jonathan Fisher, Architect and Urban Strategist at Massingbird Ltd. Taking inspiration from the distinctive Moscow Metro's own Circle Line, the intention was to emphasise that the new London Overground orbit from Highbury & Islington to Clapham junction was a natural, simple, integral part of London in the same way as the original inner Circle Line. The two circles were the starting points from which the rest of the map was designed. The River Thames was deliberately omitted to try and bind north and south London together. The Thameslink cross-London line is shown. Despite its recent upgrade for high frequency services, it still does not appear on the official map.*

If the aspiration is simple line trajectories, then higher-order linear maps almost always disappoint. Despite the extra freedom, perfect straight lines are rarely possible and the more corners that are eradicated the more those that remain draw attention to themselves. One unusual solution is to eradicate straight lines altogether, creating a curvilinear map instead. The intention with these is to minimise changes of curvature and avoid all unnecessary S-bends, so that harsh transitions are smoothed away and, whichever line is followed, the eye encounters little resistance. These design criteria are necessary to avoid wild flailing tentacles and require a lot of effort. Unfortunately users do not always appreciate this, assessing curvilinear maps as being attractive but difficult to use, even though objective measures, such as the time needed to plan a journey, do not bear this out. In general, some people like the aliveness of these creations but many object to their lack of organisation. The maps simply do not look as though they have been designed, irrespective of how much thought went into creating them.

Perhaps the most radical use of curves is to base the map on concentric circles. The existence of these designs originated from the completion, in 2012, of the London Overground orbit around central London and a number of alternatives were put forward as a means to emphasise the new connectivity. In fact, there are several different ways in which concentric circles maps can be implemented, varying by the criteria in which routes qualify for circular

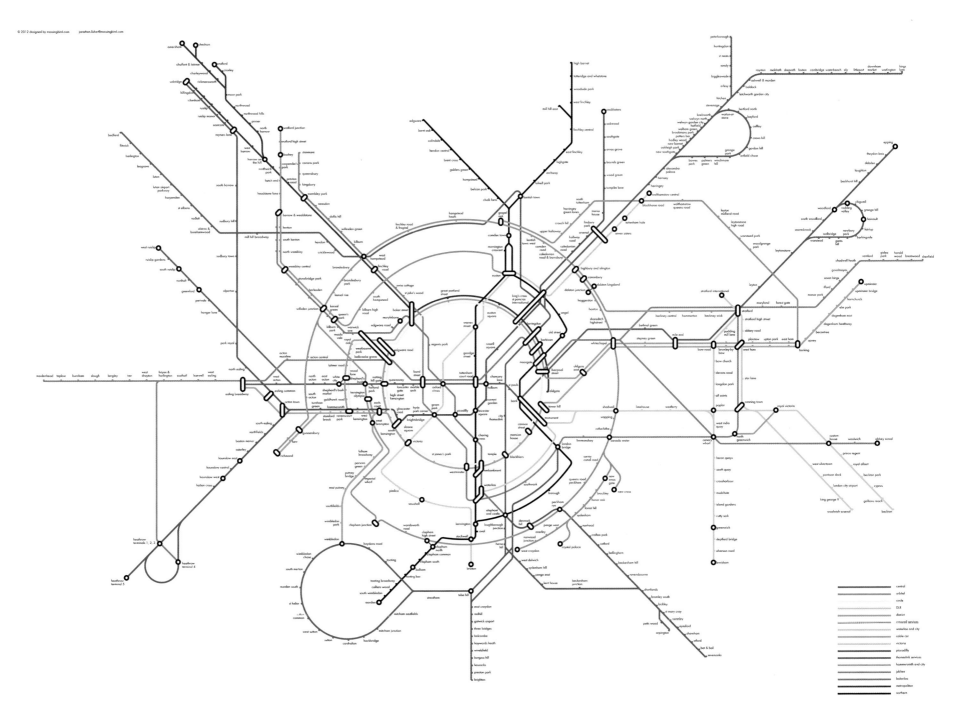

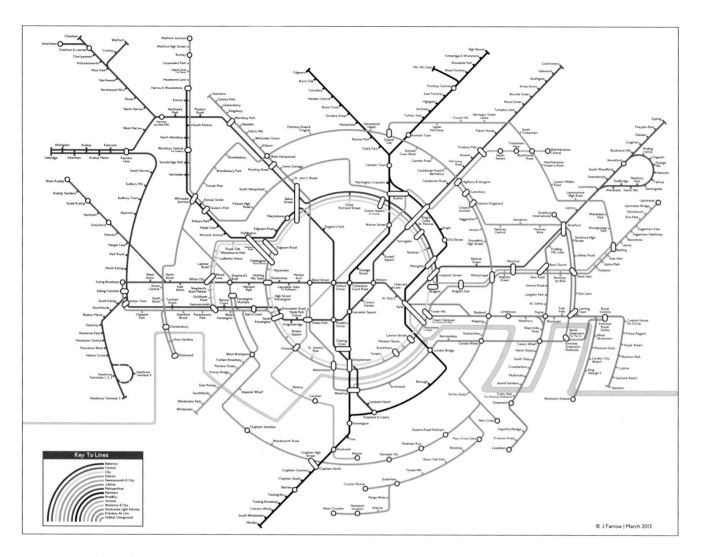

Key To Lines
Bakerloo
Central
City
District
Hammersmith & City
Jubilee
Metropolitan
Northern
Piccadilly
Victoria
Waterloo & City
Docklands Light Railway
Emirates Air Line
Orbital Overground

© J Farrow | March 2013

Left: *A concentric circles map independently designed by Jonny Farrow in 2013. This demonstrates how people working separately, with the same rules and similar priorities, can converge. Some parts of this map are similar to the one on p. 93 – where only certain solutions are feasible given the constraints – but others differ.*

Right: *In 2012 the author created a different type of concentric circles map. In order to maximise coherence, an attempt was made to relate straight lines to circles by centring every arc at the same point and radiating straight lines (spokes) from this same location. The result would be straight lines that were perpendicular to curves. The Circle Line does not respond well to being shown as a perfect circle and this forced the author to break his own design rules, so that straight lines at tangents to arcs were also permitted, and also straight lines parallel to the spokes and tangents used elsewhere on the design. As a result, the Circle Line resembles the Underground roundel, but this was a natural consequence of the structure of the network and the design rules. It was not deliberately planned. The map was meant to be a cartographic joke and was never intended to be taken seriously. Had the author known that it was going to go viral, he would have made the design less topographically distorting.*

treatment and how these relate to the other lines. Hence, straight lines might, for example, be octolinear or limited to spokes radiating from a central point. Applying the rules strictly can create powerful images, forcing city networks into unprecedented levels of organisation, but the shape of the London Underground makes it resistant to these sorts of experiments, testing the ingenuity of designers and resulting in considerable topographical distortion.

The London Underground network continues to attract the attention of designers worldwide, both amateur and professional. In the process, a rich diversity of maps has been created, ranging from barefaced impersonations to truly innovative design explorations. The network provides an ideal testbed for people who desire to investigate new concepts – it is complicated enough to be a challenge to map and yet simple enough that there is the potential for innovative approaches to make genuine improvements in usability. Of course, implementing a new map is only the first step, and claims that novel designs are easier to use should always be backed up with hard evidence rather than informal observations and anecdotes. In the interim, it is likely that we can continue to look forward to surprises in the future; creations that challenge our conceptualisations of effective information design.

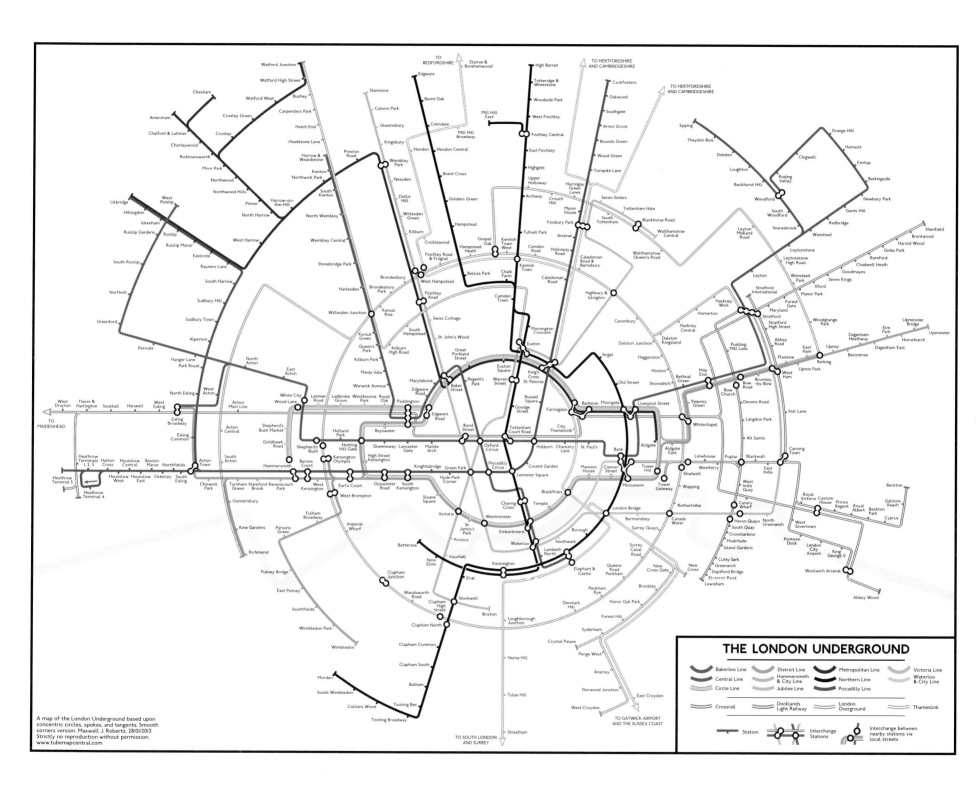

Index

Bibliography

Cerovic, J. (2017). *One metro world*. Published by the author.
Day, J.R., & Reed, J. (2019). *The Story of London's Underground* (12th ed.). Capital Transport.
Dobbin, C. (2011). *London Underground Maps*. Lund Humphries.
Dodd, J. (2018). *Maps of London's Transport*. Capital History.
Dow, A. (2005). *Telling the passenger where to get off*. Capital Transport.
Garland, K. (1994). *Mr Beck's Underground map*. Capital Transport.
Glover, J. (2015). *London's Underground* (12th ed.). Ian Allan.
Guo, Z. (2011). Mind the Map! *Transportation Research Part A, 45*, 625–639.
Guo, Z., et al. (2017). Redesigning subway map to mitigate bottleneck congestion. *Transportation Research Part A, 106*, 158–169.
Howes, J. (2000). *Johnston's Underground type*. Capital Transport.
Jerome, J.K. (1889). *Three men in a boat*. Penguin Books.
Jerome, J.K. (1891). *Diary of a pilgrimage*. Sutton Publishing.
Leboff, D., & Demuth, T. (1999). *No need to ask!* Capital Transport.
Lloyd, P.B. (2012). *Vignelli: Transit maps*. RIT Cary Graphic Art Press.
Mijksenaar, P., & Vroman, R. (1983). London Transport map: A Delft project. *Typos, 6*, 36–40.

Nöllenburg, M., & Wolff, A. (2011). Drawing and labeling high-quality metro maps by mixed-integer programming. *IEEE Transactions on Visualization and Computer Graphics, 17*, 626–641.
Ovenden, M. (2009). *Paris underground*. Penguin Books.
Ovenden, M. (2015). *Transit maps of the world* (3rd ed.). Penguin Books.
Ovenden, M. (2016). *Johnston and Gill: Very British Types*. Lund Humphries.
Ovenden, M., & Roberts, M.J. (2019). *Airline Maps*. Penguin Books.
Roberts, M.J. (2008). *Information pollution on the Underground Map*. http://www.tubemapcentral.com/information_pollution/ip.html
Roberts, M.J. (2008). *Underground maps after Beck* (2nd ed.). Capital Transport.
Roberts, M.J. (2012). *Underground maps unravelled*. Published by the author.
Roberts, M.J. (2014). What's your theory of effective schematic map design? Schematic Mapping Workshop, University of Essex, April.
Roberts, M.J. (2019). The Decade of Diagrams. 2nd Schematic Mapping Workshop, TU Wien, April.
Roberts, M.J., Gray, H., & Lesnik, J. (2017). Preference versus performance. *International Journal of Human Computer Studies, 98*, 109–128.

Roberts, M.J., Newton, E.J., & Canals, M. (2016). Radi(c)al departures. *Information Design Journal, 22*, 92–115.
Roberts, M.J., & Rose, D. (2016). Map-induced journey-planning biases for a simple network. *Transportation Research A, 94*, 446–460.
Shaw, P. (2011). *Helvetica and the New York City subway system*. MIT Press.
Transport for London Corporate Archives: LT000227/190, How to use and protect intellectual property rights of London Regional Transport.
Transport for London Corporate Archives: LT000460/247, Maps, folders, route diagrams.
Transport for London Corporate Archives: LT000728/048, Design right and copyright.
Transport for London Corporate Archives: LT001904/003, Infringement of trade mark and copyright.
Transport for London Corporate Archives: LT001904/038, Infringement of trade mark and copyright.
Transport for London Corporate Archives: LT001904/039, Infringement of trade mark and copyright.
Vertesi, J. (2008). Mind the gap. *Social Studies of Science, 38*, 7–33.